Joomla! 1.5 Cookbook

Over 60 quick and direct recipes to help you overcome
common Joomla! queries

Tom Canavan

BIRMINGHAM - MUMBAI

Joomla! 1.5 Cookbook

First published: October 2010

Production Reference: 1191010

Published by Packt Publishing Ltd.
32 Lincoln Road
Olton
Birmingham, B27 6PA, UK.

ISBN 978-1-849512-36-7

www.packtpub.com

Cover Image by Javier Barria (jbarriac@yahoo.com)

Credits

Author
Tom Canavan

Reviewer
Eric Brown

Saidur Rahman Bijon

Tahsin Hasan

Acquisition Editor
Douglas Paterson

Development Editor
Tariq Rakhange

Technical Editor
Gauri Iyer

Indexer
Tejal Daruwale

Editorial Team Leader
Mithun Sehgal

Project Team Leader
Priya Mukherjee

Project Coordinator
Shubhanjan Chatterjee

Proofreader
Stephen Silk

Graphics
Nilesh Mohite

Production Coordinator
Melwyn D'sa

Cover Work
Melwyn D'sa

About the Author

Tom Canavan has been in the Computer and IT industry for 20+ years where he spent several years as a Systems Consultant to many Fortune 100 clients and other global companies.

Canavan is considered a top security and disaster recovery expert in the Joomla! world. He is the author of the Packt Publishing book *Joomla! Web Security*.

He is a former CIO and is currently the co-founder of `SalvusAlerting.com`. Canavan contributes articles on security and disaster recovery to several websites.

It's often difficult for me, as an author to write the acknowledgements of a book. Not because I feel there's no one to thank, but because there are so many.

Firstly, I thank Jesus Christ, my Lord and Savior. Without his help, I would not have had the courage to strike out on yet another book. My deepest gratitude and thanks goes to my wife, who put up with me writing another book. Special thanks to Mike Carson of `JoomlaShowroom.com` for his assistance with understanding K2. Thanks go to Alexis at `Freakedout.co`, for helping me through some rough spots in the technology. Learning the Joomla! 1.6 ACL was no small feat and special thanks go to Jen Kramer for educating me on it. Thank you to the hardworking editors and staff at Packt who put up with multiple delays, and rewrites from me. I know there are many others who helped me and please forgive me if you didn't get a direct mention. I am very grateful for your assistance and help.

Most especially, thank you dear reader for purchasing this book. God bless you.

About the Reviewer

Eric Brown, who was born and raised in California, joined the U.S. Navy at the age of 17 and became a Preventive Medicine Technician. Upon exiting military service, he left the medical field behind and moved to Nebraska and entered into college studying art and design which resulted in a Bachelor of Science degree in Graphic Design from Wayne State College in Nebraska. Eric has since then branched out by teaching himself (or learning from others) various aspects of HTML, CSS, and PHP as well as a variety of other code languages and web marketing strategies and tools. He currently owns his own design and development business located in Curtis, NE. where he lives with his wife and pets.

Over the years, Eric has worked for a local design and development firm in Nebraska on such projects as the Golden Spike Tower website aimed at tourist traffic centered on the Union Pacific's Bailey Yard and with a premier pet industry design and development firm as a project manager. He has also written for such prestigious publications as *Trafficology* (a purchased print publication on web marketing read by over 80,000 world-wide), CMSWire.com (a leader in content management news), Revenues.com (a highly rated site on various aspects of marketing), and Gadgetell.com (a well-known gadget news site).

Eric was a reviewer for Joomla! 1.5 Javascript jQuery book from Packt Publishing. He has also been involved in other books as well as providing editing, image touch-up, and custom hand-drawn maps for Tagging Along (a Neville Family retrospective) and editing, layout, cover art, and image touch-up on My Life and Community (Biography of Ken Huebner).

I would like to thank any and all who have helped to bring my career to this point, but most of all I would like to thank my wife Jaime and two children Ariel and Autumn for all their patience and understanding as my career and business underwent their developmental stages.

Saidur Rahman Bijon is an open-source enthusiast from Bangladesh. He is a computer science graduate from BRAC University. He has been developing web applications since 2005. During this time, he developed e-commerce, web 2.0, social networking, and micro-blogging applications and he worked on Joomla!, Zend Framework, Drupal, and WordPress. He is also a Zend-certified engineer. He shares his knowledge and ideas at `http://saidur.wordpress.com`.

He started his career by developing a large-scale application for the Bangladesh Navy with a Japanese and US-based offshore company. Currently, he is working in Blueliner Marketing, LLC (`http://www.bluelinerny.com/`), an US-based company as a senior software engineer.

Saidur was a reviewer for *Codeigniter 1.7* book from Packt Publishing.

I appreciate Packt Publishing for giving me the opportunity to review this book. I really am thankful to my family, friends, and colleagues for their help.

Tahsin Hasan is a software engineer. He has passed the Zend Certification Examination on 09, August, 2009 and has become the seventeenth **Zend Certified Engineer** (**ZCE**) from Bangladesh. This is the top-most certification on PHP from Zend, the developer of this outstanding scripting language. He is a tech enthusiast and always keeps himself well-equipped with latest technologies. He has completed his M.Sc. and B.Sc. in Computer Science and Engineering from Jahangirnagar University.

Tahsin Hasan has profound knowledge on **LAMP** environment. His advanced understanding of database environments and Apache web server is an asset. He has proficiency in scalability and optimizing server performance. He has worked with Zend Framework, CakePHP, Codeigniter, and Symfony.

This book is dedicated to my best friend in the world, Carol Ann.

Table of Contents

Preface	**1**
Chapter 1: Installing Joomla!	**7**
Introduction	7
Preparing to install	8
Setting up your database on a cPanel® host	15
Setting up your database on a GoDaddy.Com® server	20
Installation of Joomla! 1.5	25
Ensuring permissions are correct	35
Chapter 2: Working with phpMyAdmin	**39**
Introduction	39
Exporting a MySQL database using phpMyAdmin	41
Importing a MySQL database using phpMyAdmin	48
Working with your database using phpMyAdmin	53
Removing a table from your database	58
Removing content from a table	61
Chapter 3: Templates	**65**
Introduction	65
Installing the template using the administrator tool	66
Replacing the default administrator template	68
Manual installation of a template	74
Using more than one template on your site	78
Determining your templates' module positions	85
Replacing a logo in a template	90
Chapter 4: Editing Content and Menus	**97**
Introduction	97
Installing a new editor	98
Setting up sections	103

Setting up categories	108
Article creation	114
Adding new menus	124
Setting up a blog on your Joomla! site	133
Adding an extension menu	141
Chapter 5: Managing Links, Users, and Media	**151**
Introduction	151
Managing users	152
Setting up a site contact	158
Working with media	163
Managing the login and user experience	169
Web Link manager	177
Changing lost super admin password	182
Chapter 6: Managing Modules and Components	**187**
Introduction	187
Installing and managing components	188
Creating menu items for components	193
Installing, creating, and managing modules	196
Chapter 7: Managing Articles Using the K2 Content Construction Kit	**201**
Introduction	201
Installation and introduction of K2	202
Working with items AKA articles	217
Working with comments	225
Summary	229
Chapter 8: Installing Third-party Extensions	**231**
Introduction	231
Installing and using eXtplorer	232
Using and configuring content uploader extension	237
jomCalendar	241
Using and configuring CompojoomComment	248
Summary	253
Chapter 9: Troubleshooting	**255**
Introduction	255
Developing a 'troubleshooting mentality'	256
Summary	266
Chapter 10: Securing your Joomla! Site	**267**
Introduction	267
Setting permissions for your site	270
Patching	270

Using .htaccess and php.ini	272
Denying specific IP addresses	279
Summary	280
Chapter 11: Joomla! 1.6	**281**
Introduction	281
Joomla! 1.6 ACL	282
Working with new category manager	292
Extensions	300
Appendix	**305**
Usernames, passwords and database reference sheet	305
Turning the legacy mode on or off	306
Changing the favorite icon	307
Setting up a site in a subfolder	308
Questions to ask a prospective host	309
Checking and updating your server software	311
Index	**315**

Preface

If you are a Joomla! site owner, you must already be aware of how this robust, easy to use, open source content management system can help you build a great looking site instantly. You must also be aware of the many problems that it can throw up from time to time. Find the solutions to all your basic and advanced Joomla! queries, so you don't have to wait for someone on the forums to help you out every time.

The Joomla! 1.5 Cookbook will provide you with quick and direct solutions to the most common and uncommon problems faced by you, the Joomla! site owner, sidestepping all the theoretical fuss.

Joomla! is the insanely popular, award winning content management system which helps you build professional looking websites, even if you don't have any HTML programming experience or design skills.

Normally, sometimes you might trip over some common pitfalls which would slow the progress of your website down. This book will help you find a direct and quick way through common problems which can be easily avoided with a few tips and tricks. It starts off with solutions to the most common queries that you might face during the installation and set up for Joomla! 1.5, then moving on swiftly to guide you through Joomla! templates, modules, security, managing your users, and much more. So the next time things go wrong with your Joomla! site and you are wondering, for example, how to work with your site's database; just pick up this book and quickly find your way through.

Find the easiest solutions to many pitfalls that might fall in the way of your Joomla! site.

What this book covers

Chapter 1, Installing Joomla!: This chapter covers the important process of installation. In this chapter, you will learn how to install and use the FTP program FileZilla. Using this you will then learn how to transfer Joomla! up to your server and ensure permissions are correct. There are several different hosting platforms you can choose, but many of them run an application known as cPanel®. Another hosting platform is from the company GoDaddy.com®. You will learn how to use both of these popular systems to install your database and configure it. The last item is a cheat sheet for you to record all the particulars for your host.

Chapter 2, Working with phpMyAdmin: As you learn in *Chapter 1*, Joomla! is a database-driven system that renders the content on the screen from database queries. In this chapter, you will learn how to export (backup) and import (restore) a database. The database is comprised of "rows" and "tables", working with those you can get fine-grained control over your systems. Lastly, you'll learn how to remove a database table or simply empty out the data.

Chapter 3, Templates: Joomla! has a special extension known as a Template. The Template is what gives the the look to the external part of your book. Using a template requires that be installated. In this chapter you will learn how to install and assign a template as your default one. Of course, templates, like the rest of Joomla!, have a bit of management that goes on and ensuring you know that will give you a sharp-looking site.

The back-end of Joomla! has a template too, known as the administrator template. This template can be replaced with any number of third-party templates available for this purpose. You will learn how to install and assign that one as well.

There are times when you want to use more than one template; this will be covered along with learning how to change a logo (graphics) in a template. Finally, templates use a 'module' position to determine where to show content. You'll wrap up this chapter with knowing how to determine a template's MODULE positions.

Chapter 4, Editing Content and Menus: Joomla! is a Content Management System, and thus has a host of things such as an editor, sections for content, and putting content into categories. You will learn in this chapter how to install an editor, set up, and define the sections and categories that match your needs. Creating an article is the heart of Joomla! - that is - providing something for your visitors to read or interact with. We cover this as well as setting up menus to display the content.

You may want to use Joomla! for a blog site. Joomla! is perfect for this and we wrap this chapter up with instructions on setting up a blog site on Joomla! and learning how to add an extension menu.

Chapter 5, Managing Links, Users and Media: With your Joomla! site you will likely be managing users. This chapter covers all the administrative detail such as adding, deleting, and suspending users. It covers how to take your users and assign them into Groups. You can change or edit the login for your users to match your business requirements.

You're likely to have a need for your clients to reach out to you. Publishing your e-mail is unsafe due to spammers gathering it. Joomla! has provided a means to create a contact using specific users. You'll go through the steps to set up and configure this user.

Adding in links to your site from external sources gives you a great source of extra content. This process is known as using Web Link manager.

Finally, should you ever find yourself having lost your admin password or been locked out of your administrator console, you'll need to manually reset the password for your database. We wrap up this chapter with a simple and quick means to do so.

Chapter 6, Managing Modules and Components: Joomla! can be extended via the use of "Extensions". These extensions fall into three categories: Components, Modules, and Plugins. This chapter covers the installation and management of components and modules. Additionally, you will learn how to create the necessary menu items to drive these applications.

Occasionally, you will need to enable, disable, or uninstall an extension. This step is simple and is covered in a brief recipe.

Lastly you will learn how to change the menu order of components.

Chapter 7, Managing Articles Using the K2 Content Construction Kit: K2 is a wonderful content creation kit from `Joomlaworks.gr`. K2 gives you the ability to manage content in an extremely powerful way. In this recipe, you'll learn how to install and configure K2. Using a short cut known as a 'master category', you can templatize your settings in K2 and greatly ease your administration time.

K2 offers some great extras such as connections for YouTube and PhotoGalleries as well.

If you add K2 to an existing Joomla! site, you don't have to recreate all the articles. K2 offers an import feature and you'll become very familiar with it here.

Like Joomla!, K2 also offers categories, except that it removes the concept of Sections. What that opens up is Categories, within Categories, within Categories. This is known as Nested Categories. This recipe will show you how to set up and configure your categories for maximum use.

Tag Clouds are a popular means to display descriptions about your content and help with your Search Engine Efforts. You'll learn how to use this powerful tag cloud system.

The final two recipes cover configuration and moderation of comments in K2 as well as some tips and tricks to enhance your K2 experience.

Chapter 8, Installing Third-party Extensions: In this recipe, you'll be introduced to a few popular third-party extensions. The extensions are: eXtplorer, the Content Upload extension, JomCalendar, and CompoJoom comment system for Joomla! Each of these adds a unique level of functionality that rounds out your site.

Chapter 9, Troubleshooting: You will run into trouble from time to time with your Joomla! site or server. This chapter helps you with establishing a good and well-known troubleshooting process and offers some assistance on specific problems such as connecting to your database.

Chapter 10, Securing your Joomla! Site: Security is one task you should spend an appropriate amount of time and not skip. This set of recipes will assist you through the proper setting of permissions - a common trouble spot. You will learn how to patch, or in other words update your code. Apache web server provides a special setting file called `.htaccess` that allows you change and configure many important parts of your site. You'll learn how to use `.htaccess` to protect your site.

From time to time you may have a directory that you wish to keep private, free from prying eyes. In the recipe, *Preventing Unauthorized Directory Viewing*, you'll learn how to stop access to unauthorized persons.

Hackers love sites that give lots of error information, this helps them learn what your site is running and potentially gives them a clue on breaking in. You'll build a universal error page that gives the information on errors to your visitors that prevents hackers from learning too much.

Rounding out the security chapter, you'll discover how to disable your servers "banner", (a means to divulge important) information, block IP's and evil bots as well as adding protection for PHP, the language Joomla! is written in.

Chapter 11, Joomla! 1.6: Joomla 1.6 is the newest (and at this time, still beta) version of Joomla!. This is essentially a new version from the ground up. There are many new and powerful features in 1.6, such as the Access Control Level system or ACL. You'll spend time learning how to set up and configure this as well as establishing certain ways to restrict content.

Users and groups have changed a bit in 1.6 from the previous version and getting familiar with them will help you adopt v1.6.

The next two recipes are on learning to control access on a per article basis and using the new category manager. Lastly, there have been a great number of improvements in the extension manager and you'll discover those in the final recipe of this chapter.

What you need for this book

You will need your desktop or notebook computer with an Internet Browser. You'll need to have or obtain a FTP client program, such as FileZilla. It will be beneficial to download the application known as NotePad+. This is a Windows application that replaces the normal notepad application.

The other technologies used in this book include the Linux operating system, MySQL database, PHP, and the Apache Web Server. You will only need a web hosting account with those installed on this.

The final piece is the most recent version of the Joomla! 1.5.xx family and optionally the latest version of Joomla 1.6!.

Who this book is for

If you are a Joomla! site owner and have some problems that you want to get rid of quickly; or you just want to get particular things working or improved, this is the book for you. HTML, CSS, or programming knowledge is not required.

Conventions

In this book, you will find a number of styles of text that distinguish between different kinds of information. Here are some examples of these styles, and an explanation of their meaning.

Code words in text are shown as follows: "If you see this on your particular setup be sure and upload the fles into the folder called `public_html`."

A block of code is set as follows:

```
SetEnvIfNoCase User-Agent "^libwww-perl*" block_bad_bots
Deny from env=block_bad_bots
RewriteEngine On
RewriteCond %{HTTP_USER_AGENT} ^BlackWidow [OR]
RewriteCond %{HTTP_USER_AGENT} ^Bot\
```

New terms and **important words** are shown in bold. Words that you see on the screen, in menus or dialog boxes for example, appear in the text like this: "Click the **New Site** button".

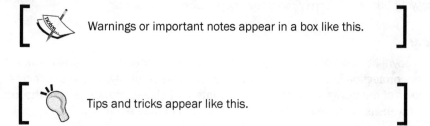

> Warnings or important notes appear in a box like this.

> Tips and tricks appear like this.

Reader feedback

Feedback from our readers is always welcome. Let us know what you think about this book—what you liked or may have disliked. Reader feedback is important for us to develop titles that you really get the most out of.

To send us general feedback, simply send an e-mail to `feedback@packtpub.com`, and mention the book title via the subject of your message.

If there is a book that you need and would like to see us publish, please send us a note in the SUGGEST A TITLE form on www.packtpub.com or e-mail suggest@packtpub.com.

If there is a topic that you have expertise in and you are interested in either writing or contributing to a book, see our author guide on www.packtpub.com/authors.

Customer support

Now that you are the proud owner of a Packt book, we have a number of things to help you to get the most from your purchase.

Downloading the example code for this book

You can download the example code files for all Packt books you have purchased from your account at http://www.PacktPub.com. If you purchased this book elsewhere, you can visit http://www.PacktPub.com/support and register to have the files e-mailed directly to you.

Errata

Although we have taken every care to ensure the accuracy of our content, mistakes do happen. If you find a mistake in one of our books—maybe a mistake in the text or the code—we would be grateful if you would report this to us. By doing so, you can save other readers from frustration and help us improve subsequent versions of this book. If you find any errata, please report them by visiting http://www.packtpub.com/support, selecting your book, clicking on the errata submission form link, and entering the details of your errata. Once your errata are verified, your submission will be accepted and the errata will be uploaded on our website, or added to any list of existing errata, under the Errata section of that title. Any existing errata can be viewed by selecting your title from http://www.packtpub.com/support.

Piracy

Piracy of copyright material on the Internet is an ongoing problem across all media. At Packt, we take the protection of our copyright and licenses very seriously. If you come across any illegal copies of our works, in any form, on the Internet, please provide us with the location address or website name immediately so that we can pursue a remedy.

Please contact us at copyright@packtpub.com with a link to the suspected pirated material.

We appreciate your help in protecting our authors, and our ability to bring you valuable content.

Questions

You can contact us at questions@packtpub.com if you are having a problem with any aspect of the book, and we will do our best to address it.

1
Installing Joomla!

In this chapter, we will cover:

- Installation of an FTP program
- Transferring Joomla! files to your server
- Setting up and test of your database on a **cPanel® server**
- Setting up and testing of your database on a **GoDaddy.Com® webserver**
- Installation of Joomla! 1.5 on your webserver
- Ensuring permissions are correct
- Cheat sheet for access information

Introduction

Installation of Joomla! 1.5 is typically very simple. While there are very few choices in hosting you need to make to install Joomla!, many users are tripped up by some common pitfalls. This chapter will help you avoid those. This chapter will show you how to install Joomla! on two different but common types of hosting platform.

We will look at setting up the database on two common hosting platforms, cPanel® and GoDaddy.com®. Both of the hosting systems offer various and important features, yet each accomplishes setup of your database in a different manner.

In this chapter we will be covering:

- Setting up of the database
- Getting the necessary details from your database server
- Logging in to the database to ensure it's working

The first host type we'll cover is a cPanel® based host, which is found in many, many hosting platforms. The examples we use are from the popular host `http://www.rochenhost.com/` which hosts `Joomla.org`

The other hosting platform we discuss is `GoDaddy.com®`.

Each approaches the task of the database setup very differently, yet they accomplish the same goal - setting up your database for Joomla!.

Once you get past the hurdle of setting up the database on the host, then the steps to install Joomla! are the same. This chapter will show you how to install an FTP client, set up each host, and then how to setup Joomla! 1.5.

Our first recipe is setting up the **FTP (File Transfer Protocol)** using an Open source application called FileZilla. You will use the FTP program to transfer the Joomla! 1.5 source files from your local machine to your server.

There are a few decisions you will need to make and space has been provided in this chapter to record your settings for future reference.

If you write down your settings be sure and keep this manual in a safe place. Loss or exposure of these settings could result in your site being damaged or attacked by a third party. Think of your ATM PIN - this is just as important.

Joomla! has a few requirements such as username, passwords, language, and whether or not you wish to implement the FTP layer.

Getting it wrong the first time is not the end of the world and is easily fixed by reinstalling or by correcting the install. See the chapter on Troubleshooting for more information.

Downloading the source for Joomla! should only take a few minutes and opening it is easy on most any Modern Windows® or Macintosh® Machine.

Grab a pencil and paper and let's get started.

Please note `GoDaddy.com®` is a registered trademark of GoDaddy.com, Inc. & cPanel® is a registered trademark of cPanel, Inc. `Rochenhost.com` is trademark Rochen Ltd.

Preparing to install

In this task we will gather the required materials for installation. You will need an FTP program, such as FileZilla, to upload Joomla! and other items.

Getting ready

- Get FileZilla by visiting their site at this link: `http://filezilla-project.org/download.php`

- Save it to a place on your computer that you can recall. If you are a Windows user, please select the first RECOMMENDED choice labeled: `FileZilla_3.3.2_win32-setup.exe`

If you are on a Macintosh please locate the appropriate FTP transfer program.

- Download the latest FULL PACKAGE version of Joomla! 1.5.xx from the following URL: `http://www.joomla.org/download.html`

Versions may vary

However, by the time this book went to print the current version is 1.5.21. You will see the .15 version in some graphics. Do not be concerned as they operate the same. Be sure and download the latest version for the 1.5.xx family available.

- Contact your host for your particular FTP settings. You will need:
  - ftp server address (typically `ftp.yourserver.com`)
  - Username for your ftp server
  - Password for your ftp server

Security Tip

If you cannot keep this book in a safe place do not write your production settings in here. If someone gains access to your settings you wrote down, it could result in someone gaining unauthorized access. A full sheet has been provided in the appendix for you to fill in and tear out should you need to.

For convenience you may record those settings here:

FTP SERVER OR IP ADDRESS: _____

FTP USER: _____

FTP PASSWORD: _____

FTP PORT (OPTIONAL): _____ (typically PORT: 21)

- Admin information for your Joomla! installation

For convenience you may record those settings here:

Admin: The default user name is **ADMIN** - for installation that is what you will use.

Password: _____

eMail account: _____

[
Did you know..
FTP is not considered the most secure means to communicate with your server. In the chapter on security you will be introduced to a more secure means of communication called SSH.
]

Depending on your host once you set up and login with FTP you may have to navigate to the website directory (known often as `public_html`). Ask your host to set up your FTP account to point to the path to the web sites root directory as default.

How to do it...

1. Install FileZilla by double-clicking on the executable. This will take about two minutes.

   FileZilla is very self explanatory and accepting the defaults is the best method to get it installed and working.

   Once installed, it will launch and you should see this screen:

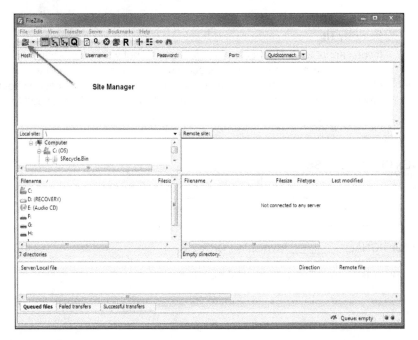

2. We will need to set up your FileZilla client to talk to your server.

   Click **File | Site Manager**

   You will now see the following screen:

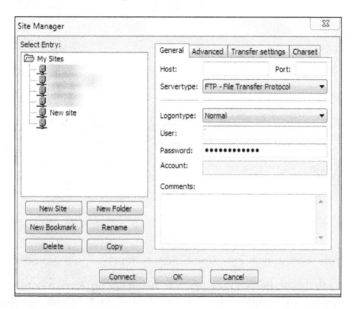

3. Setting up **Site Manager**

   This will open up the configuration for a new HOST entry.

4. Click the **New Site** button

   You will need the FTP settings you wrote down previously.

   - ❑ **HOST**: Enter the your FTP information that your host gave you
   - ❑ **PORT**: Enter port number your host gave you (typically 21). *Note this is in most cases automatically handled for you by FileZilla and you should not need to change it.*
   - ❑ **Servertype**: Leave as **FTP - File Transfer Protocol** unless instructed by the webhosting provider to use a different setting
   - ❑ **Logontype**: Select **Normal** (it will default to **Anonymous**)
   - ❑ **User**: Username that your Host gave you
   - ❑ **Password**: The password your host gave you
   - ❑ **Account**: Leave this blank

5. Click **Connect** to save and test the connection. It should show you something like the following screenshot:

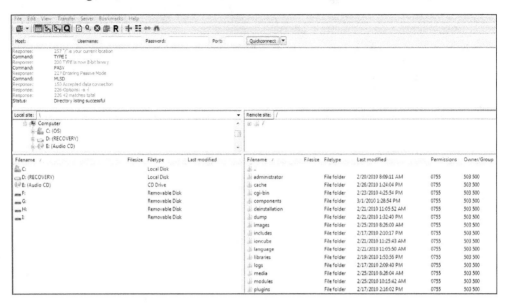

Once you see this screen you are ready to begin set up. Please note that the contents on your screen's right and left windows will be different. You should see a folder listing on the right screen of your contents.

  If you do not see this screen it means your connection was refused by the server. Repeat the above steps. If it still fails, contact your host and verify the settings.

6. Uncompress Joomla!

    Locate the compressed (zipped) file you downloaded in Item 2. It will be named like this: `Joomla_1.5.XX-Stable-Full_package.zip`(code in text) where "xx" represents the latest version of Joomla! you downloaded.

    Using Windows® right-click the file and choose **Extract All...** - this will uncompress the file into a folder by the same name. It is worth noting that other applications such as WinZip, WinRAR or others will handle this procedure differently.

    Record Joomla! path name here: _____

  Zip
You may have a program installed such as WinZip® on your computer - this is a terrific tool for uncompressing the files. Using it will produce the same results.

7. Start FileZilla

   Start your FileZilla application (if it is not already) and open **Site Manager**, select your host, and click **Connect**.

8. Navigate in the FileZilla window titled: **Local** site to your uncompressed Joomla folder. You should see something like this: (Note that is the left window of FileZilla)

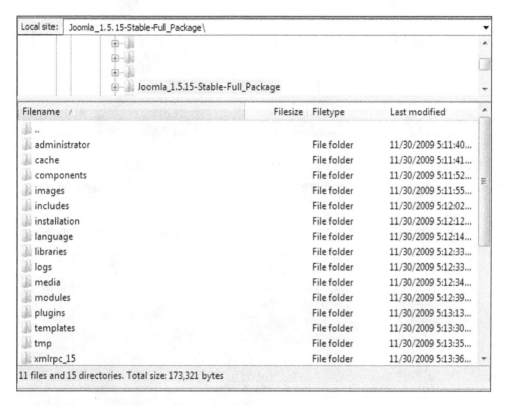

Local site:	Joomla_1.5.15-Stable-Full_Package\			

	Joomla_1.5.15-Stable-Full_Package			

Filename /		Filesize	Filetype	Last modified
..				
administrator			File folder	11/30/2009 5:11:40...
cache			File folder	11/30/2009 5:11:41...
components			File folder	11/30/2009 5:11:52...
images			File folder	11/30/2009 5:11:55...
includes			File folder	11/30/2009 5:12:02...
installation			File folder	11/30/2009 5:12:12...
language			File folder	11/30/2009 5:12:14...
libraries			File folder	11/30/2009 5:12:33...
logs			File folder	11/30/2009 5:12:33...
media			File folder	11/30/2009 5:12:34...
modules			File folder	11/30/2009 5:12:39...
plugins			File folder	11/30/2009 5:13:13...
templates			File folder	11/30/2009 5:13:30...
tmp			File folder	11/30/2009 5:13:35...
xmlrpc_15			File folder	11/30/2009 5:13:36...

11 files and 15 directories. Total size: 173,321 bytes

9. This is a screen showing you what is on your machine.

10. Transfer files over from your local machine to Server

11. Left-click one of the folders in your **Local site** window, it will be highlighted.

12. Next press *Ctrl+A* to highlight all of the folders.

13. Right-click on the highlighted folders and you will see the following screen:

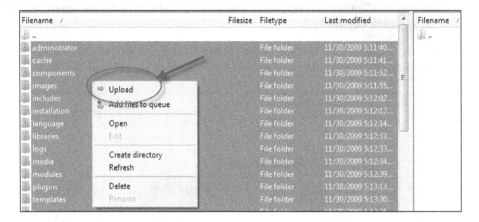

14. Click the **Upload** button, as circled in the preceding screenshot.

You will see the files copying to the RIGHT window. Once done, you will see this in the right-hand pane, which represents your server.

The following is a screenshot of your web server after Joomla! has been uploaded.

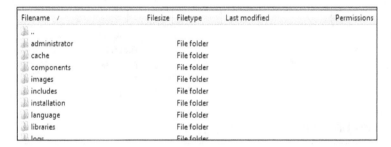

What is public_html?

On some web servers you may see a folder called `public_html` and a folder called www. If you see this on your particular setup be sure and upload the files into the folder called `public_html`.

This completes the upload process. Next step - establish the database on your host.

How it works...

FileZilla, in this example, is being used with the FTP protocol. FTP has to have two computers to setup and conduct a transfer. The "server" itself, in our case, the web server, has FTP server software running on it. It will accept a session from a client, (FileZilla) and allow the user to add/change/delete/copy files and execute other commands.

Given the sensitive nature of FTP, it can be a security risk; therefore, strong passwords are the only choice you should make. In addition to that, turning off **Anonymous FTP** is vital. Anonymous means, "ANY" FTP client can connect and execute commands such as deleting all files, or uploading viruses. Always make sure you disable **Anonymous FTP**.

Setting up your database on a cPanel® host

This recipe will guide you through the steps necessary to set up a database on your cPanel® enabled host. cPanel® is by far one of the most popular control panels for web hosting, and as you get to know it you will see why. It is a very powerful and well-built application. We'll refer to it several times through various recipes.

We are using a `http://www.rochenhost.com/` server for our screenshots.

Setting up your database is simple and easy.

Getting ready

To get started you were provided login details by your host for your cPanel® or 'hosting control' - most likely they will have their own name for it. However if you login and see something like the following generic cPanel screenshot - you are in the right place:

cPanel® is trademark by cPanel, Inc.

If you are in doubt, ask your hosting technical support.

Gather your host login information:

Login URL for cPanel®: _____

Username for cPanel®: _____

Password for cPanel®: _____

If you cannot keep this book in a safe place, do not write usernames and passwords in it. These should be kept in a safe place.

Each database needs to have a unique name. You will need to provide a name for the database, the user name (for Joomla! itself), and a password. These should be different to your other username and passwords. It is recommended that you allow cPanel® to generate the password for you. This will ensure you have a very strong password.

How to do it...

1. Login to your cPanel®

2. Scroll down your screen till you see **DATABASES**

3. Click the icon **MySQL® Database Wizard** - it should look this:

4. After you click this you will see the following screenshot - this is where you will start the database creation. In this example we have a "prefix" of **watcher_** you will have a different prefix.

5. Fill in your database name which can be anything you want. It has a limitation of 16 characters. Try to choose something descriptive but not common. Write the database name here:

   Database name _____

6. Click the **Next Step** button

   You should see something like:

   MySQL® Database Wizard

   Added the database watcher_cookbook.

   This indicates our database **watcher_cookbook** was added successfully.

7. Create a user for Joomla! in our database

    This step is necessary for Joomla! to talk to the database.

8. Create a username no longer than seven characters.

    Record the username here _____

    Now - for maximum security use the password generator. It will create a strong password for you. Here is an example of it in action.

9. Once it generates a password for you, click the **I have copied this password in a safe place** checkbox to use it.

    Record the password here for later use: _____

    Once you complete this step you should see this screen with your username inserted:

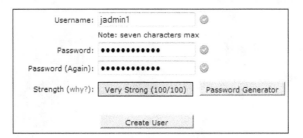

10. This completes the creation of the user. In our case we chose **jadmin1** and our password of **U&{u$.S1F2t_**.

11. Give the newly created user rights to use the database.

    The next screen you will see is the **Privileges** screen.

    The **Privileges** screen defines the rights this user will have to the database.

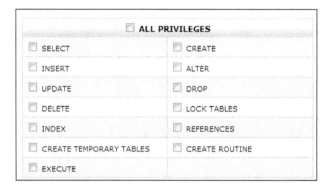

12. Check the **ALL PRIVILEGES** box.

    Now you will see that all the boxes are checked as follows. If they are not checked, Joomla! will fail to install properly.

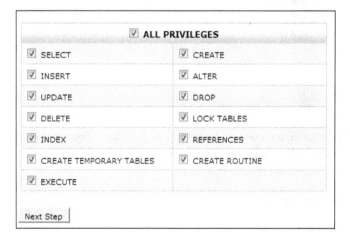

13. Click the **Next Step** button. You will be presented with a screen similar to the following:

> User watcher_jadmin1 was added to the database watcher_cookbook.
>
> Add another database
>
> Add another user using the MySQL Databases Area
>
> Return to Home

This completes the setup of your database. Now click **Home** in the upper left of the screen.

There's more...

We need to be sure the database is working. We do that by returning to the main cPanel® page and scrolling back down to the **Database Section**. Look for this icon and click it:

Once you click that icon it will launch the administration tool for MySQL. You will see a screen like the one following this paragraph. Please note your information will be different, and the count in your database will be ZERO (0). This partial screenshot shows we have two databases in our example setup. You will only have one.

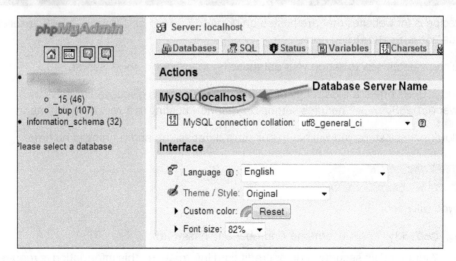

Note the circled text in the preceding screenshot. The portion following the word MySQL will be your database server name.

[*Your server name may differ but will likely be localhost*   ]

Record the information you see located in your version of cPANEL®.

Database Server Name: _____

[**Database Server Name Tip**

Most of the time, you can simply use `localhost` as your Database Server
Name unless you see something else indicated in the green circled area.   ]

This completes the set up of your database on cPanel®. You may skip over the `GoDaddy.
Com`® instructions and continue with installing Joomla!

How it works...

This GUI that is embedded into the cPanel interface issues the necessary MySql commands
to instruct the database server on setting up a database, adding a user, and giving that user
proper permission to use the database.

Setting up your database on a GoDaddy.Com® server

This recipe is for websites that are hosted on `GoDaddy.com`® or `GoDaddy.com`® resellers
such as `PotentiaHosting.com`™.

These steps detail how to set up your database on a `GoDaddy.com`® server.

`GoDaddy.com`® offers a wide range of tools equal to the tools discussed in previous section.
However `GoDaddy.com`® handles setting up your new hosting in a very different manner.

By following these steps you will have your site's database up and running in no time.

Getting ready

What you will need:

- ▸ `GoDaddy.com`® username / number and password
- ▸ Your four digit security code or credit card information - this information is required
  should you need to contact technical support.

How to do it...

1. Login to GoDaddy.com® using your username and password.

2. To reach the database setup, we have to navigate through the menu. Follow these steps:

3. Click **Hosting**.

4. Under **My Products** choose **Hosting** - this will take you to the control panel:

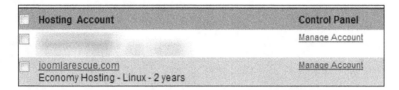

The preceding screenshot shows (in our example) two accounts - yours will show the number of accounts you have purchased.

5. Now click on **Manage Account** next to the **Hosting Account** you wish to set up.

6. You will be taken to the Hosting Control Center control panel - choose **Databases** - you will see the following icon.

7. Once you click the MySQL icon you are taken into the set up system. Click the **Database** button on the upper right:

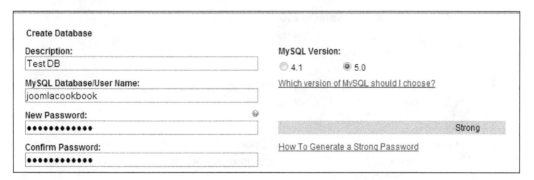

8. This screen is where you will enter all your information.

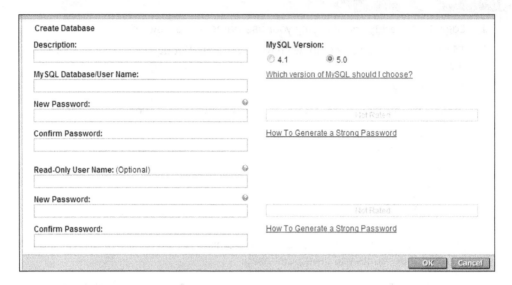

9. How to complete this screen:

   ❑ Provide a **Description** (example: Joomla! 1.5 website)

   ❑ Provide a **MySQL Database/User Name**. Note that on GoDaddy. com® this means both the database name and the Username are identical. This will be important for your Joomla! installation

   ❑ Create a strong password and repeat it. See the tips GoDaddy. com® provides for creating a strong password - labeled **How to Generate a Strong Password**.

   ❑ For our purposes you can leave the **Read-Only User Name**, **New Password/Confirm Password** sections blank

   ❑ Choose **MySQL Version 5.0**

   ❑ Click **OK**

 It is important that you select 5.0 as your database. 4.1 is provided for older applications that cannot support the new database.

10. The next step on GoDaddy.com® can take a few hours in some cases. So don't panic if it states **Pending Setup** for a very long time. You will see a screen like the following until the database is set up:

5.0	joomlacookbook		Test DB	Pending Setup	

11. In your database list (see the preceding screenshot) once it is complete click the pencil icon on the right:

Clicking this will provide the critical details you will need to set up Joomla! You should see a screen similar to the one shown in the following screenshot:

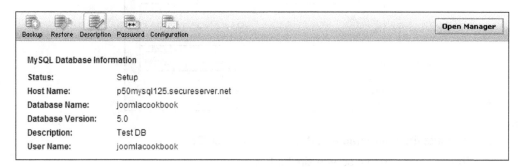

12. Record your details here:

    Status: Should read **Setup**

    Host Name: _____

    Database Name: _____

    User Name: _____

    Password: _____ (optional as you should have recorded it earlier)

13. Check database to ensure it is working

    On the same screen you are currently looking at, click **Open Manager** in the upper right corner:

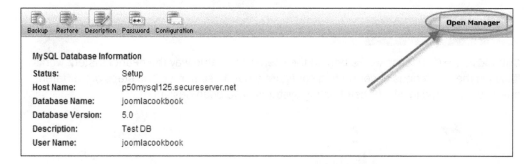

This will open the database manager for you. You will see the following screen and you will need your **Username** and **Password**:

14. Populate the **Username** and **Password** and click **Go**.

This will take you to a screen similar to this:

You will see on the left your database under **information_schema**. It should say (0) next to it. In our case it reads: **joomlacookbook(0)**.

This indicates your database is set up. In the next recipe you will install Joomla!

How it works...

GoDaddy.com® process works behind the scenes the same way the cPanel system works. It issues the commands to set up and configure a database server. The steps are different due to the method in which their hosting systems have been designed.

Installation of Joomla! 1.5

You are now ready to install Joomla! 1.5 on your web hosting platform. In this recipe, we will go through the set up of your database and uploading of the files.

This process should only take about five to ten minutes to complete. Once done you will have a working Joomla! site ready to add your own content, templates, extensions, and more.

Most of this process is handled through your browser.

Getting ready

You will need:

- ▸ User name for database
- ▸ Password for database
- ▸ Database server name
- ▸ Site name
- ▸ Email address for Admin of the site
- ▸ Site admin password
- ▸ FTP client (FileZilla or other) and FTP user name and password

How to do it...

1. Open a browser and point it at your domain or IP address.

   Example: `http://www.MyDomain.com`

   `http://192.168.1.100`

   This will trigger your Joomla! installation script to start up. You will see this screen:

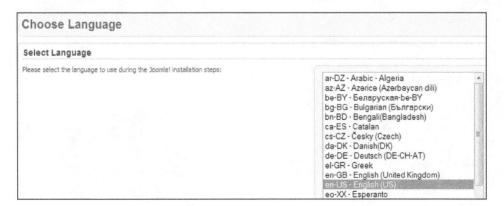

This is the initial start-up screen for Joomla! 1.5 installation. It defaults to English (US), However Joomla! is available in many languages.

2. Please choose your language or click **Next** to accept the default.

3. **Pre-Installation Check**

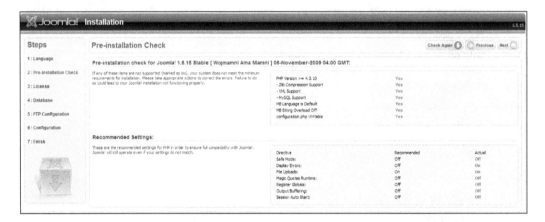

This is the **Pre-Installation Check** screen. You should see all green in the top box and mostly or all green in the lower box. Here is a screenshot of the server's setup options close up:

4. In this case we have **Display Errors** turned **On**, it is recommended to be **Off**.

A closer look will show you each screen.

PHP Version >= 4.3.10	Yes
- Zlib Compression Support	Yes
- XML Support	Yes
- MySQL Support	Yes
MB Language is Default	Yes
MB String Overload Off	Yes
configuration.php Writable	Yes

The **Recommended Setting** screen is a follows:

Directive	Recommended	Actual
Safe Mode:	Off	Off
Display Errors:	Off	On
File Uploads:	On	On
Magic Quotes Runtime:	Off	Off
Register Globals:	Off	Off
Output Buffering:	Off	Off
Session Auto Start:	Off	Off

You should see all green **Yes** here, if you do not contact your host and tell them to adjust your settings. In our example we have purposely turned **On Display Errors**. You likely will not see it in your installation. However you should follow the recommended settings for maximum performance.

5. Once you get all green **Yes** and your actual settings match the **Recommended** settings, repeat step one or press this button on top of the screen:

6. Should these be set differently, you can change them in a file called php.ini. I recommend you speak to your host about changing them should they be different.

   This will rerun the checks. If however everything is ok, then move to the next step.

7. License review.

This is an information screen showing the GNU/GPL license that applies to your use of Joomla!.

8. Read the license and click **Next**.

9. **Database Configuration**

   This is the screen you will use to configure your database settings.

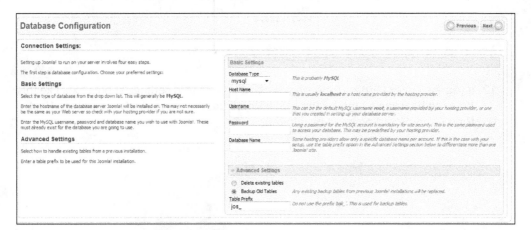

10. This is a partial screenshot of the database configuration screen. You will need to enter your details in the following screenshot:

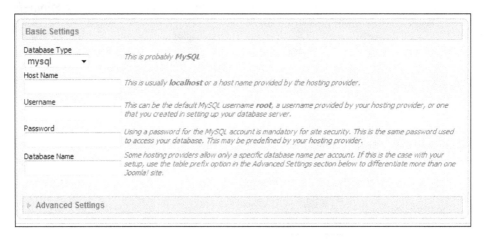

In this screen you will need the database settings you set up in the previous recipes. You will see two versions of the same setting. One demonstrating GoDaddy.Com® and the other representing cPanel®.

11. The following screenshots are part of the database configuration screen. The different examples are shown to demonstrate GoDaddy.com® versus cPanel®

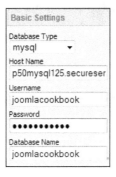

12. If you are on GoDaddy.com® your installation for basic settings should look like this. Note the **Username** and the **Database Name** are the same. And it has a long **Host Name**. Your Host Name will be different.

13. If you are on cPanel® your settings example will look more like this. Note that in most cases **localhost** will be your **Host Name** and the username and database name should be different from each other. Again your answers will vary.

14. Now fill in the **Basic Settings** screen with the correct responses.

15. Do not click **Next** yet.

16. Database configuration continued.

    Under basic settings you will see **Advanced Settings** as follows:

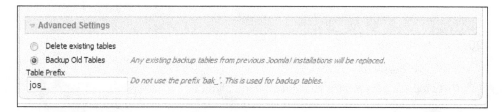

    Assuming this is a new installation, then no action is required on your part.

17. FTP Layer (THIS STEP IS OPTIONAL AND SHOULD BE SKIPPED IF YOU DO NOT NEED IT)

    On some hosting setups there are various technical reasons why you cannot change permissions or upload extensions that are important to the operation of the site. This layer, while optional most of time is crucial for those hosting setups.

    Contact your host and ask them specifically if they are running 'SuExec'. If so, you can skip this step.

    For GoDaddy.com® or Potentiahosting.com you should not need to install this layer and can skip this step.

18. You will need the following information to complete this setup:

    ❑ **FTP User**

    ❑ **FTP Password**

    ❑ **FTP Root Path** (the directory where your website will reside)

19. You can save the FTP password but for security it is recommended you DO NOT. To save your password, click **Yes** under the **Advanced Settings**.

    Do not change the Host or Port information.

20. Click **Next Step**

21. Main configuration

    This step will personalize your Joomla! installation.

    You should be on this screen:

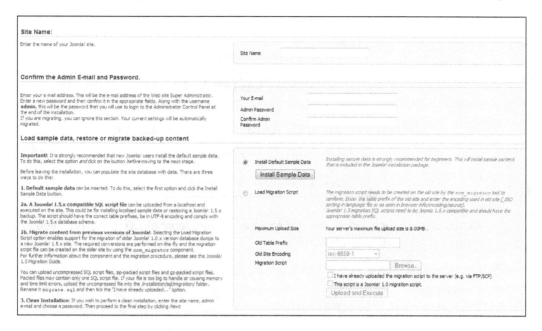

There are only a few steps here.

22. Fill in your website's **Site Name**:

This will display in the browser and search engines. Don't worry - you can change it anytime.

23. Next fill in your (admin) email and password. You must type your password in twice.

24. Now the next step is optional but recommended as this is to assist you in learning. If you are going to use your site for production, you may wish to skip this step.

The **Install Sample Data** will install a lot of menus, content, categories, and sections.

25. Click the **Install Sample Data** button:

This step only takes a few moments. You will see this upon success:

As this is a new installation, and not a migration from Joomla! 1.0 you do not need to install the LOAD MIGRATION SCRIPT.

26. Click the **Next** button.

27. Completion.

Once you complete the previous step you will be greeted with the following screen:

The text in red is giving you final instructions:

DO NOT CLOSE THIS SCREEN OR NAVIGATE AWAY.

28. Now - Open FileZilla and connect to your web server. In the right-hand pane of FileZilla, you should see a screen similar to the following:

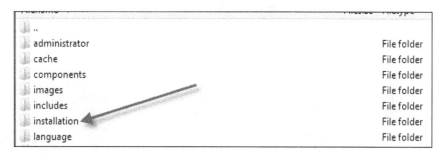

29. Highlight and right-click the **installation** folder. You will see the following screen.

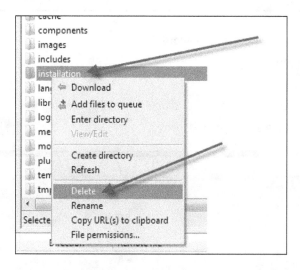

30. Click **Delete** for the **Installation** folder. This will take a few moments. Once done, close FileZilla and return to your Joomla! installation.

31. Now you can click the **Admin** button and login:

You should see this screen:

32. Enter your **Username** and **Password**.

33. This will log you in.

34. Press **Logout**.

35. Close and reopen your browser and open your new website (`www.yourdomain.com`)

36. This is how your website should look.

This completes the installation and testing of your new setup.

How it works...

This installation program sets up all the necessary parts of the system. It will place all the proper information in the various database tables. It writes out the ever important **CONFIGURATION.PHP** file which provides the instructions to Joomla! on how to access your database, and a few other important settings.

See also

If you have an older Joomla! 1.0 site, you may wish to migrate it to a 1.5 site. You can learn more about migration from the following URL. Personally I recommend building your new site from scratch to prevent any compatibility problems.

```
http://docs.joomla.org/Migrating_from_1.0.x_to_1.5_Stable
```

Ensuring permissions are correct

In any computer, files and programs have a 'permission' level, meaning it states who can read, write, change, or run them. In Joomla! (Linux-based machines) we have three sets of permissions: one for the 'owner', one for the 'group', and one for the 'world'. A common security mistake is setting these incorrectly.

In this short recipe, you will check your permissions for your 'files' and 'folders'.

Getting ready

You will need:

Your FileZilla FTP client and FTP username and password.

How to do it...

1. Open your FileZilla FTP client and in your **Site Manager** select your web host
2. In the right-hand pane of FileZilla, you will see your files and folders. To the far right (scroll over) you will see the **Permissions** and **Owner/Group** columns as shown in the following screenshot:

Permissions	Owner/Group
0755	503 500
0755	503 500
0755	503 500
0755	503 500

There are many files and they should be set (as this is a fresh install) ok. However, it won't hurt to check.

3. Click one of the folders then (for Windows ® users) press *Ctrl+A*. This will highlight all the files and folders in your site. You should see a screen similar to the following:

This partial screenshot shows you have selected everything.

4. Right-click in the blue colored portion. Select **File permissions**...:

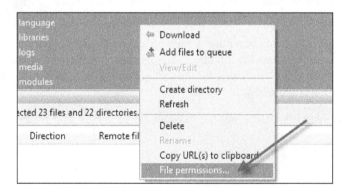

5. **FOLDER PERMISSIONS** should be set for **755**.

   The following items should be checked or filled in:

6. **Numeric value** should be set for **755**.

7. Check the box **Recurse into subdirectories.**

8. Check the box **Apply to directories only**.

   Note that if you get it wrong, don't worry - you can repeat it.

   This process will take a few minutes so be patient.

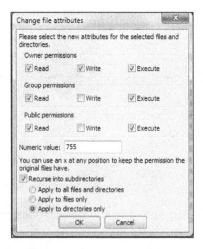

9. File Permissions should be set to **644**

 In some hosting setups you may not be able to perform this step. This would be why you would have needed to turn on the FTP LAYER earlier

10. Following the same process as in step 4, highlight all your files and folders, right click, and click your file permissions selection.

    This time however you will change the settings as follows:

11. **Numeric value** should be set for **644**.

12. Check the box **Recurse into subdirectories**.

13. Check the box **Apply to files only**.

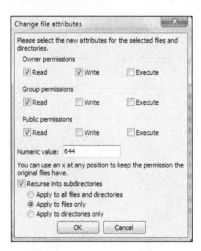

This step will take longer than the **DIRECTORIES** step.

Once complete you may exit FileZilla.

How it works...

This will establish the 'permission's properly. Linux sets up three different classes for permissions on each file and folder:

User (u): This is the owner of the file

Group (g): Other users who are in a group and able to access files

Other (o): PUBLIC or the WORLD (meaning - everyone who does not belong to the other two roles)

You noted the numbers 755 and 644. These numbers are represented by the OCTAL numbering system (BASE 8). What they tell the Operating System about the files is as follows:

READ is   4

WRITE is   2

EXECUTE is   1

In OCTAL we add them the same as normal numbers. For example, 4+2+1 = 7. Meaning we give the OWNER of the folder READ, WRITE, and EXECUTE permissions.

Whereas we give the GROUP and OTHER 4+1 = 5, READ and WRITE permission.

On our FILES we give the OWNER 4+2 = 6 and for the GROUP and OTHER we give 4 only - giving them permission to READ ONLY.

2
Working with phpMyAdmin

In this chapter, we will cover:

- ▶ Exporting a database
- ▶ Importing a database
- ▶ Working with database rows and tables
- ▶ Removing a table
- ▶ Emptying a table

Introduction

In the first chapter and recipes, you were shown how to setup a database and establish users. The tool for driving this is called, phpMyAdmin.

phpMyAdmin is a popular, open-source tool that is a standard on most web hosts. Written in PHP, it enables you to handle all the administration of your MySQL database, keeping you from working in the command-line mode.

Here is an example of a command for setting up a new user:

```
CREATE USER 'jcookbookadmin'@'localhost' IDENTIFIED BY 'MyPassword';
```

or creating a database

```
CREATE DATABASE jbookdb;
```

or assigning privileges to it

```
GRANT ALL PRIVILEGES ON 'jbookdb' . * TO 'jcookbookadmin'@'localhost';
```

As you can see, attempting to remember all those commands is probably more than you want or need.

As Joomla! is primarily a database-powered system, from time to time you will need to know your way around phpMyAdmin for some of the tasks you may face.

One important item that phpMyAdmin can help you with is **exporting** your database. What this means is backing up your database and putting it in a safe place.

In later chapters, you will learn how to install and use tools to assist with backup and recovery; however in an emergency having knowledge of this tool is important.

This tool can also be dangerous and I STRONGLY RECOMMEND, you backup your database (using export) before you try anything. That way you can quickly restore it.

Before diving in, let's learn some terms that are used in describing databases.

Term	Description
Table	A table is a 'container' that holds records or rows. Your data resides in those rows.
Row	A container within a table that defines how your data is stored
Browse	This command enables you to browse through your data in your database, viewing it by table, by row, or row by row. In other words, you can see all the Joomla! data.
Data	This is your actual data. Think of names, address, phone numbers, and so on. This in a phone book would be considered the 'data' of the phone book. In your Joomla! database, your 'content' would be the data.
Drop	A powerful and dangerous command. Allows you to drop a 'table' or 'tables' in a database. Be careful - there is NO undelete.
Empty	This empties a table of its contents, but preserves the table.
Export	This will export the data in a single table or the entire database. There are several formats you can choose from. For most cases, you will choose SQL format. This is also known as a DUMP.
Import	This is the reverse of export. It brings data and data structures into the database. This will create a new table and associated structures. It can overwrite existing tables.
Manage MySQL users and privileges	Gives you the ability to add, change, delete users, and their privileges.

Exporting a MySQL database using phpMyAdmin

Backing up your database is critical to long term safety and reliability of your Joomla! site. Should the database become corrupted or get damaged, having a copy to restore is vital.

In this recipe we will "export" or "backup" our database.

Exporting is the process of making a copy and saving it locally on your desktop or other means of storage.

Getting ready

You will need your username and password for accessing your database in your control panel. Depending on your hosting you may need your username and password for the database.

How to do it...

1. Log in to your hosting and navigate to your cPanel®.
2. Locate your **phpMyAdmin**.

3. Click the **phpMyAdmin** button to open. You will see a screen like the following:

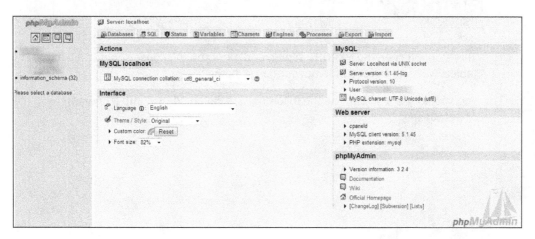

4. Choose your database

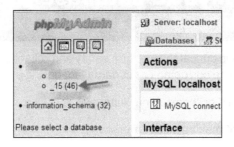

In our example, we're clicking the database _15. You will need to choose your database. The next screenshot will show a screen that should be similar to yours.

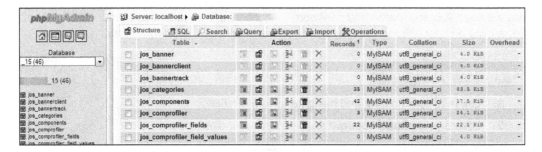

This is a view of all the rows and tables in our database. Your screen will scroll down to show them all.

5. Click the **Export** button.

This step will open the **EXPORT** screen and allow you to choose some or all of the tables. Now you will see a demonstration of both.

You should see a screen like the following. It is called: **View dump (schema) of database**

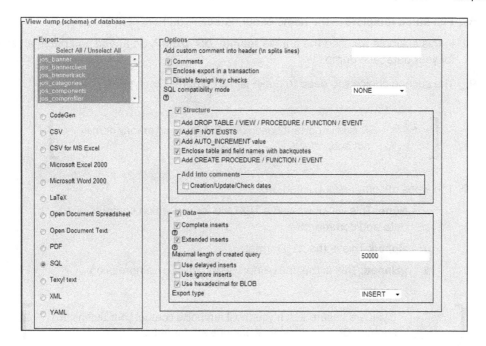

For our purposes keep the defaults.

6. In the upper left-hand side, under **Export** click **Select All**.

   This will highlight all the tables as you can see as follows:

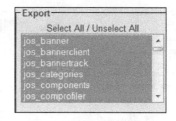

7. At the bottom of the screen you will see this image:

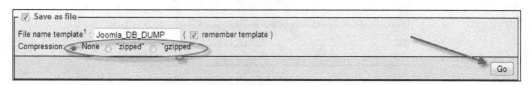

There are three parts we need to pay attention to.

8. **File name template** is the name of our database dump.

   In this example we used the phrase **Joomla_DB_DUMP.** Go ahead and put in a name for your database dump.

9. The second choice you need to make is the compression type.

 This is important based on what your server may or may not support.

10. The types of compression listed are:

   ❑ **None**: This will download a TEXT file for you which contains all the data and commands

   ❑ **zipped**: This is the Zip format

   ❑ **gzipped**: This is the linux/unix version of Zip compression

 If you are unsure which your host supports contact your technical support. Or consider saving one of each formats.

11. In this example, choose **zipped** format and click **Go**.

   Depending on the browser you use, your screen will look something like this. In this case, I'm using Firefox.

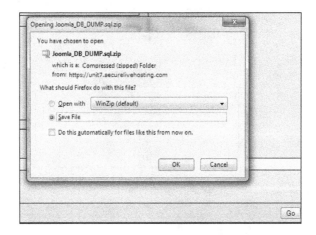

12. Click **OK** to accept the zipped file. BE SURE AND REMEMBER WHERE YOU SAVE IT. Again each browser has a different default location it stores to. Firefox and Chrome use a folder called Downloads. It varies greatly depending on your Operating System and browser.

13. This particular process of exporting a database is very helpful in case of the event where you want to move your site to a new server or a new database server. You are strongly encouraged to exercise EXTREME CAUTION when working inside the phpMyAdmin tool. It's a simple matter to accidentally delete your database. `<line break><line break>`Next let's learn what each checkbox does on this screen.

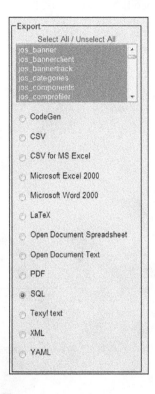

14. **Export** allows you to choose ALL or SOME of the tables in the database.
    In this example, we see the following "tables".

    - **jos_banner**
    - **jos_bannerclient**
    - **jos_bannertrack**
    - **jos_categories**
    - **jos_components**
    - **jos_comprofiler**
    - **Jos_banner**

    There are many more as you scroll down that list.

Below that are several 'radio buttons' to choose the output type that the database will provide you. The default is **SQL**. However, as you can see there are many types, such as creation of a PDF File, an Excel® file, and many others. Each of those is useful for different purposes and most have options specific to their format.

For our purposes we will use the default of SQL.

The next part of the screen is called **OPTIONS**. This is where you will control various items in your **Export** also known as "**DUMP**". We will use the term Export and DUMP interchangeably.

15. This is the left-hand side of the screen.

    The first portion is for the addition of 'comments' into your DUMP. As a normal matter of course you should not need to change that part from the defaults.

16. **Structure** will probably share the same chosen options. Let's look at each.

    ❑ **Add DROP TABLE/VIEW/PROCEDURE/FUNCTION/EVENT**: As you can see this is NOT checked. If you CHECK THIS, it will INSERT into your DUMP (backup) the necessary commands to tell the database to drop (erase) anything in it that matches what is in the backup. If you leave it UNCHECKED it will not. As a matter of course, I check this on a backup. That way I am ensured that when I do a restore it will remove any broken or wrong parts of my database and replace them with the correct data.

But what if..?

If you use the DROP command, and your "**backup**" is bad or corrupt, you will only restore something bad or corrupt. It is important to note, that the procedures to download a database are the same procedures to use to make a backup. Downloading a copy is a backup.

□ **Add IF NOT EXISTS**: This is a default item (and should remain checked) that will add the necessary commands to "add" the content (data) back to the database IF it does not exist. This is helpful if you have a blank database.

The next two defaults that are checked are:

□ **Add AUTO_INCREMENT**

□ **Enclose table and field names with backquotes**

These are necessary for proper insertion. They should remain checked.

□ **Add CREATE PROCEDURE / FUNCTION / EVENT**: This box by default IS NOT checked. You most likely will not need to check it. This will add back in a "stored procedure" or other advanced database concepts that are beyond the scope of this book.

17. The next portion of the screen directly below is: **Data**.

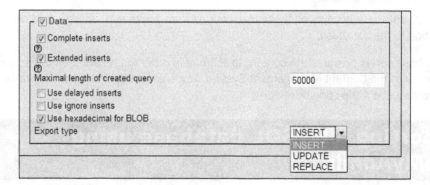

As you can see the DATA box is checked already, as well as **Complete inserts** and **Extended inserts**. An "INSERT" is the command that will be included with your data dump that tells the database to "INSERT" or write it in when it's imported (that is, uploaded or restored).

In most cases the box **Maximal length of created query** should be fine at 50000, so we'll leave it.

Timeout

In the case of a LARGE database, your database server may time out giving you an error message. Checking this will put in the proper commands in your dump to instruct the database server to give it more time (in essence it delays the writes to the database server). For a deeper technical explanation of delayed inserts see: `http://dev.mysql.com/doc/refman/5.1/en/insert-delayed.html`

18. The next two boxes are to be left in the state you see in the preceding screenshot.

One point to note is the drop-down box on the lower right in the above image shows three different commands we can embedded in our database dump. We want **INSERT** for our purposes. However, there is also **UPDATE** and **REPLACE**.

UPDATE: If used would 'update' the data in a table and row

REPLACE: It works exactly like **INSERT** except that it will overwrite anything in its path

For our purposes accept the default setting that are presented.

How it works...

The MySQL database accepts all these instructions from you to add, change, and delete information to the database.

The database server provides the content to Joomla! in order to present it on the screen. This is the power of the Content Management System. You are managing the content, rather than being worried about the code development.

Importing a MySQL database using phpMyAdmin

In the event of a problem, such as corruption of data, or loss of the database, it may be necessary to restore your database. This is known as importing.

Importing is the process of putting copy back into a database. This is also known as restoring.

Getting ready

You will need your username and password for accessing your database in your control panel. Depending on your hosting you may need your username and password for the database.

How to do it...

IMPORTING:

1. Login to your hosting and navigate to your cPanel®.

2. Locate your **phpMyAdmin**.

3. Click the **phpMyAdmin** button to open. You will see a screen as follows:

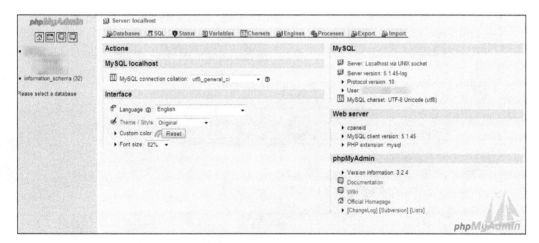

4. Select your database

 For the purpose of demonstration, a blank database has been created. However the steps to IMPORT are the same.

The database in this case is being indicated by the arrow.

5. Once you click on your database if it contains tables and rows, you will see a number next to it and all the tables on the left side of your screen.

    In our case, we have a new (empty) database and we see:

6. You will see a message (not shown in image) that states **No tables found in database**, and the count next to the database name is zero (0).

    This database is now ready for IMPORT of the data from the EXPORT step.

7. Click the **Import** button found on the top toolbar.

    The **IMPORT** function will display a simple screen as follows. Please note, for publishing purposes, this is a partial screenshot:

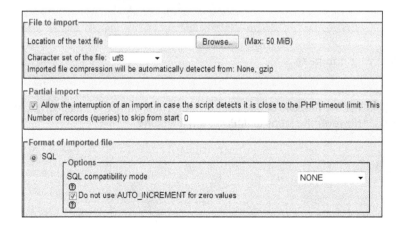

It is important unless otherwise directed, to accept the defaults for this screen.

8. Click the **Browse...**button in the previous screenshot.

You will be presented with a dialog box such as this one. Find the location of your EXPORTED dump file from the previous recipe and choose it, then move to the next step.

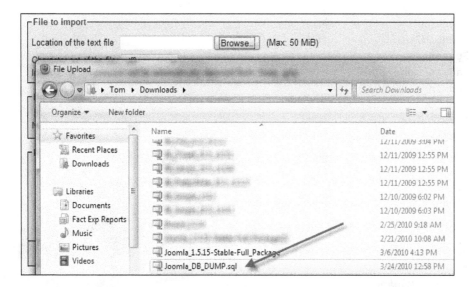

9. Click the **Go** button in the lower right-hand corner.

The database **IMPORT** will commence and should only take a few seconds.

Once done you should see a screen similar to the following one. The key thought you need to know is the number of records. In our **EXPORT**, we had forty-six records. As you can see in the following screenshot we have the same amount. Making sure the numbers are the same is important.

10. This completes our **IMPORT** operation.

How it works...

The IMPORT function works by giving the database several commands, such as the following:

```
INSERT INTO `jos_components` (
`id`,
`name`,
`link`,
`menuid`,
`parent`,
`admin_menu_link`,
`admin_menu_alt`,
`option`, `ordering`,
`admin_menu_img`,
`iscore`, `params`,
`enabled`)
 VALUES (
1,
 'Banners',
 '',
0,
0,
 '',
'Banner Management',
'com_banners',
0,
'js/ThemeOffice/component.png',
0,
'track_impressions=0\ntrack_clicks=0\ntag_prefix=\n\n', 1);
```

This tells the database to "insert" or write into the TABLE **jos_components** columns, the data that follows the VALUES key word.

 Insert is a database command that instructs the database to 'Insert' or put into, new ROWS, or content, into your database tables.

In the IMPORT process (depending on our EXPORT settings) it will execute any other commands it finds in your .sql file.

Another example:

```
CREATE TABLE IF NOT EXISTS `jos_bannertrack` (
   `track_date` date NOT NULL,
```

```
    `track_type` int(10) unsigned NOT NULL,
    `banner_id` int(10) unsigned NOT NULL
) ENGINE=MyISAM DEFAULT CHARSET=utf8;
```

The command `CREATE TABLE IF NOT EXISTS jos_bannertrack` instructs the database server to create a new table called **jos_bannertrack**. Insert would be used to put content into the table.

The great thing for restore is the `.sql` file will contain the proper commands to rebuild the heart of your Joomla! site, which is the database.

Working with your database using phpMyAdmin

This recipe will show you some basic commands and operations you may need from time to time.

I strongly suggest you setup a test Joomla! site and test database to learn these commands. That way if you break something, you won't damage your production site.

In this section we'll look at a few basic commands and scripts you may need from time to time.

Getting ready

You will need the passwords for:

- FTP
- cPanel
- Possibly your database (this can be obtained from `configuration.php`)

Depending on your hosting you may need your username and password for the database. Some hosts require it once you get into their control panel system and others do not. `GoDaddy.com`®, for instance, requires you to enter a username and password to interact with your database. Other webhosts do not require it, once you are logged into cPanel.

You will need a copy of your database (see the preceding warning). You can use the previous chapter on creation of a database and the two previous recipes to EXPORT your data and add it to a new database using the IMPORT.

How to do it...

1. Getting a list of names, username, and their email address from your database.

2. Open your phpMyAdmin and navigate to your database as in previous steps.

   Here is a screenshot of our database ready to work on.

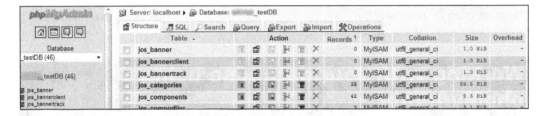

3. Click **Query** on the toolbar on the top in phpMyAdmin and click the **SQL** button.

   You will see this screen:

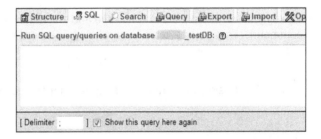

4. In the **Run SQL query/queries on database _testDB**: enter this script by typing it in and clicking **Go** in the lower right-corner.

   ```
   SELECT name, username, email
   FROM jos_users;
   ```

   This will yield the following from my test database. You will have different information in yours.

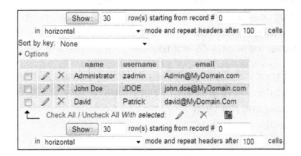

This 'queried' the database for this information and provided it quite simply.

5. Let's look at another query - one that will tell us WHO is the SUPER ADMINISTRATOR in our website. This has multiple implications, such as security and recovery of a lost Super Admin password.

    Return back to this screen by clicking the **SQL** button again.

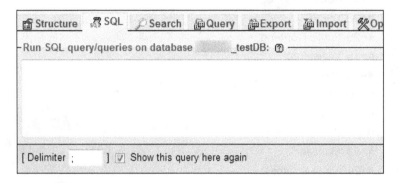

6. Enter the following script:

    ```
    SELECT name, username
    FROM jos_users
    where GID=25;
    ```

7. The GID of 25 represents the default Super Admin user. Running against our database reveals not one but TWO super administrator users.

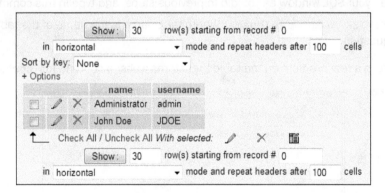

What about other GID's?

Other user GID numbers can be found by replacing the GID=25 with GID=#. For instance you can review whose who using the above SQL statement with these GID's:

#=17 'ROOT'

#=28 'USERS'

#=29 'Public Frontend'

#=18 'Registered'

#=19 'Author'

#=20 'Editor'

#=21 'Publisher'

#=30 'Public Backend'

#=23 'Manager'

#=24 'Administrator'

#=25 'Super Administrator'

8. Optimize table(s): On a very busy website, you may see performance dropping. This is a quick means to clean up the database. This script will be presented in two forms, command line, and GUI.

    Please make sure you EXPORT your database before attempting this command.

9. Open your SQL window as you did in previous steps, and type in this command:

    `OPTIMIZE TABLE tablename`: Where tablename is the name of the table in question.

10. Here is a real example on the table that stores website content, **jos_content**.

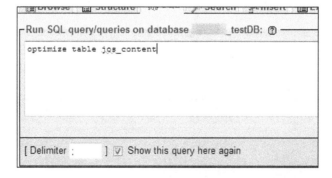

This will then show you a screen similar to the following:

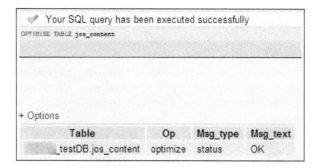

The second method allows you to optimize a single table, any number of tables, or all the tables at once.

11. Click on the DATABASE <name> link at the very top. See the arrow in the following screenshot. This will return you to the starting point for your database. In this example **testDB**.

You should see a list of all the tables as follows:

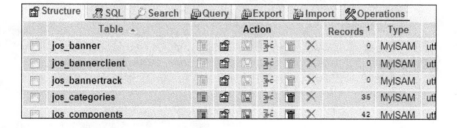

12. Scroll all the way down to the bottom, you'll see this:

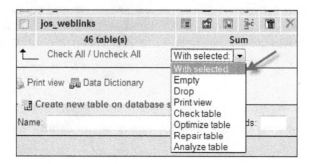

13. For convenience, the drop down has been opened for discussion.

14. Now click **Check All**, this will highlight all the tables.

15. Pull down the drop-down box.

16. Click **Optimize table**.

    You can also optimize just a single table, for instance, **jos_content**. This is a quick and easy to way to do so without having to remember SQL commands.

How it works...

Running `OPTIMIZE TABLE tablename` solves this problem. You should run the OPTIMIZE command occasionally on a busy website. 'Optimize' reclaims the space that was consumed by the deleted data.

During the operation of a website, if you have lots of content or other items changing frequently, this can leave gaps in the tables. This means your server will have to work harder, taking longer to deliver information, thus you could experience website slow down.

Removing a table from your database

Occasionally you might experience a Joomla! extension that does not uninstall properly. This can happen for many reasons and if it needs to be removed, it must be removed manually. Other instances might be where you uninstalled an extension, but it left behind its tables intentionally yet they need to be removed for any number of reasons.

This is an ADVANCED and DANGEROUS task. Using this command will result in the data in question being permanently removed from your database. BEFORE USING THESE COMMANDS BE SURE AND BACKUP (export) YOUR DATABASE

In this recipe we will look at the **command line** method to delete or remove a table. The term is 'drop' which means delete or remove. We will remove an imaginary extension table from our database called **jos_Corn_Syrup**. The situation is we have removed our extension called Corn Chart, used to track the corn fields for farmers. However, the programmer wrote our extension so that it purposely leaves behind the tables for upgrades, and so on. This is a common (and good) practice.

Getting ready

You will need your username and password for accessing your database in your cPanel® and your FileZilla client.

Depending on your hosting you may need your username and password for the database.

You will need a copy of your database (see the preceding warning). You can use the chapter on creation of a database and the two previous recipes to EXPORT your data for safety.

How to do it...

1. Open your phpMyAdmin and navigate to your database as in previous recipes.

    This time we'll start with the GUI method then move to the command line method.

    You should be in the TABLE view as follows:

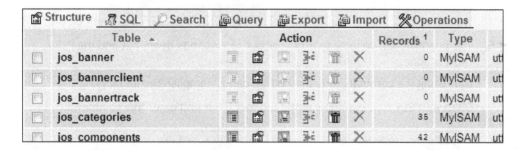

2. Scroll down till you find the TABLE you wish to drop. In our case it will be **jos_Corn_Syrup**.

    This is what we would see in our database:

    As you can see I have "checked" the box.

3. Now scroll down to the bottom and open your drop-down screen as follows:

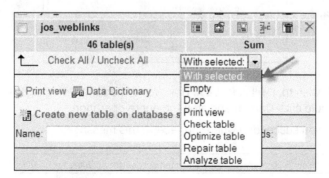

Be sure you have ONLY selected the table you wish to drop. If you have ANY OTHER table selected it WILL be dropped and will no longer be available.

In this example, we have **jos_Corn_Syrup** as the only box checked, so we click the **Drop** command in the above table. MySQL will warn you and give you a chance to verify you DO WANT to drop [erase, delete] the TABLE.

4. If you clicked **Drop** by accident, or if you changed your mind, then click **No**. In our case however, we want to DROP the tables. Selecting **Yes** in the lower right-hand side of the screen will drop the tables.

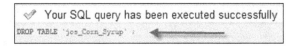

5. The phpMyAdmin console tells us that our request has been met and the table is gone.

Now using the command-line method we can accomplish the same thing.

Open your SQL query window at the top menu bar and enter this command:

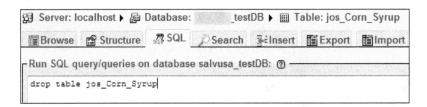

6. Click the **Go** button in the lower right to commence. You will be prompted to verify you wish to drop that table.

7. As we DO wish to, I will select **OK**. However if I had the wrong table or changed my mind, I could click **Cancel** and stop the entire operation.

You know you succeeded when you receive this message:

Here you have successfully removed a table.

How it works...

The commands we executed using the GUI are the same commands a database administrator might use managing the server. These commands tell MySQL to drop, which means permanently erase, the tables, and all the data. It's important to always backup your database before dropping a table in the event you chose the wrong one.

Removing content from a table

There might be times you wish to remove JUST the data from a table, such as if a spammer inserts names into your mailing database, or you wish to remove all of the data from any table. There are many times this might come in handy.

You will see how to delete a single row of data and delete the entire data set from the table.

In any case, the same warnings apply.

 BACKUP YOUR DATABASE BEFORE YOU START!

Getting ready

You will need your username and password for accessing your database in your cPanel® and your FileZilla client.

Depending on your hosting you may need your username and password for the database.

You will need a copy of your database. You can use the recipe to EXPORT your data for safety and backup.

How to do it...

1. Navigate to your main database menu. You should be here:

Once again we will review the GUI method first, then the command-line method.

2. Locate your table of choice - we'll once again use **jos_Corn_Syrup** as our table. In this example, we WANT to wipe out the data, but not actually remove the table from the database.

3. Choose your table as above then scroll down to the bottom of the screen till you see this screen (opened for the screenshot):

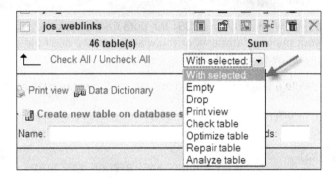

4. Choose **Empty** from the above list. This will prompt you and ask if you are SURE you wish to. Choose **Yes** in the lower left-corner of the screen to EMPTY (also known as **TRUNCATE**) the table.

    Once done you will see:

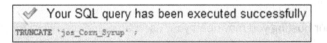

    This shows that the table was 'emptied' out.

    Command line version of Empty (known as Truncate)

5. Go back to the top of your phpMyAdmin screen and select the **SQL** button and enter this command (with the table you want):

    ```
    TRUNCATE `jos_Corn_Syrup`;
    ```

    This will ask you to verify it, and if it's correct, click **YES** in the lower right-hand corner.

How it works

This command instructs the database to REMOVE the contents by erasing the data.

In reality the "truncate" command that is called 'drops' the entire table and recreates it but without data.

However, it will maintain the structure of the database. This is useful in situations where you are developing a site and want to remove the content before you turn it over to a client, or in situations where the data is not needed but the table setup by the extension is.

See also

`http://www.packtpub.com/` offers a title for a more extensive training on phpMyAdmin - `http://www.packtpub.com/phpmyadmin-3rd-edition/book`

3
Templates

In this chapter, we will cover:

- ▸ Installation and assignment of templates
- ▸ Management of templates
- ▸ Replacing the administrator template
- ▸ Using more than one template on your site
- ▸ Determining your templates' modules' positions
- ▸ Replacing a logo in a template

Introduction

Joomla! has the ability to change its look and feel using a special extension known as a **Template**. There are hundreds, if not thousands, of templates available, and each can be customized for your use.

Don't see what you need? You can build your own or create artwork and have a template developer take your artwork and create a template that is unique to your needs.

The purpose of the template is to place your content into special sections on the screen known as **module positions**.

You can install as many templates on your site as you like and even assign a different templates to different portions of your site.

In this chapter, you will learn how to install your template, assign one as the default, and make changes to it.

So grab a template and let's get started.

Installing the template using the administrator tool

The Joomla! Administrator allows for installation of all extensions and templates to your Joomla! site. There are two means by which to install your template and in this method we will show you the most common and preferred method, using the admin console.

Getting ready

You will need to have acquired your template of choice for this step. Please note that the template will be in a compressed form. It could have a `.zip` or `.tgz` extension.

You will need the following items:

▸ Your new template's compressed file (it will contain several files)
▸ Your FileZilla or other FTP client

How to do it...

You probably purchased or downloaded a free template from one of the many sources on the Internet.

You will login to your Joomla! Administrator, then select the installation manager, and upload the template.

1. Login to Joomla! Administrator. You reach the Joomla! Administrator by typing in `http://www.YOURDOMAIN.COM/administrator`. This will prompt you with the following screen:

2. Enter your **Username** and **Password**. You will be in the Administrative Console.

3. Open **Install manager**.

4. Click **Extensions | Install/Uninstall**.

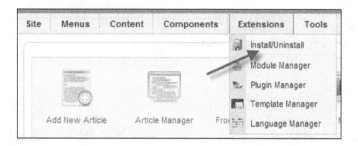

The next screen you see is the installer for Joomla!:

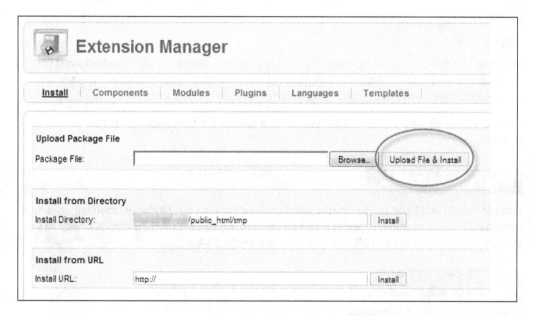

This is Joomla! universal installer. You will install all extensions and templates through this panel.

5. Click the **Browse...** button indicated by the green circle in the preceding screenshot and locate your template ZIP file, and click the **Upload File & Install** button.

    This will initiate the installation of your template, once complete you should see the following screen:

This completes the automated installation of a template.

How it works...

In this brief introduction, you uploaded a template to your site. You may have noticed if you downloaded a template, it came in a compressed form with a .zip extension. The template designers create all the necessary parts and deliver it in this fashion.

Joomla! can unzip and install this file based on a special file that tells it where to place everything.

There's more...

Occasionally, if you have permissions issues on your server, you may have trouble installing a template. This will manifest itself in a variety of ways, mainly with WRITE errors. Check to see that your folders are set to 755 and your files are set to 644.

See also

Manual installation of templates.

Replacing the default administrator template

As you have likely become acquainted with the administrative console in Joomla!, you may not have realized it is also a template. And as such, it can easily be replaced. There are a number of administrative templates available, and a few sources are listed at the end of this recipe.

Getting ready

You will need to have acquired your administrator template of choice for this step. Please note that the template will be in a compressed form. It could have a `.zip` or `.tgz` extension.

You will need the following items:

▸ Your new administrator template compressed file (it will contain several files)

▸ Your FileZilla or other FTP client

How to do it...

1. Login into the Joomla! Administrator backend and login by entering your **Username** and **Password**.

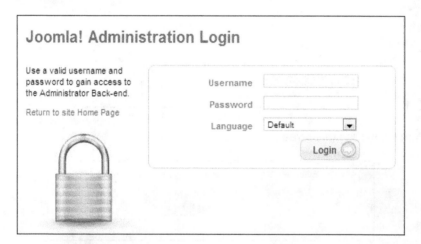

2. Review your administrator templates that are currently installed. Navigate your top menu to **Extensions | Template Manager** and click **Template Manager**.

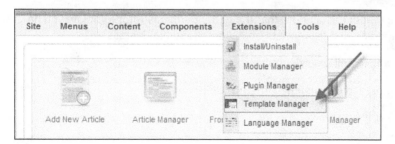

Once **Template Manager** is open you will see the following screenshot. This, by default, shows all the FRONT-END or PUBLIC templates for your site. You will want to see the administrator templates installed.

You can see a list of your installed templates as shown in the following screenshot.

3. Click **Administrator** as indicated in the following screenshot:

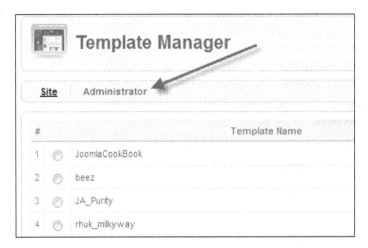

You should see this screen:

This shows you that the base administrative template, **Khepri** is installed, and is the default template. This will always be the case if there's one template.

The reader should note that the default administrator template you have been using is the one that is standard on ALL fresh Joomla! installs.

Now to install a new administrator template.

4. Navigate to **Extensions | Install/Uninstall**

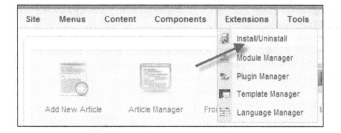

This will open the **Install Manager**.

The next screen you see will see is the installer for Joomla!:

5. Click the **Browse...** button indicated by the green circle in the preceding screenshot and locate your administrator template ZIP file, and click the **Upload File & Install** button.

This will initiate the installation of your new administrator template, once complete you should see the following screen:

6. Again, navigate on your top menu to **Extensions | Template Manager** and click **Template Manager**.

7. Select **Administrative Templates**.

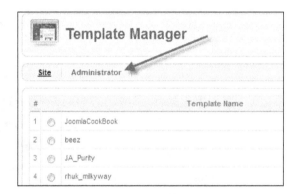

You will now see the NEW administrator template available for use. In our case, we installed the **AdminPraise 2** administrator template.

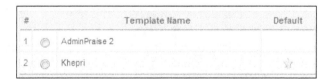

Now we need to select it as our default administrative template.

8. Click the radio button next to the **AdminPraise 2** template.

After you click the radio button, select **Default** (marked with a star) in the upper right-hand corner:

We have to complete a final step for this template by clicking **Configure AdminPraise**. Your options will vary based on the template you chose.

Now that we have it completed, here is a beforeshot of our Administrator: DEFAULT administrator template

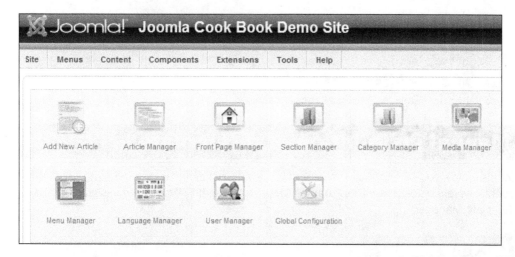

And after we install **AdminPraise 2** administrator template from AdminPraise.com and assign it, we'll see this:

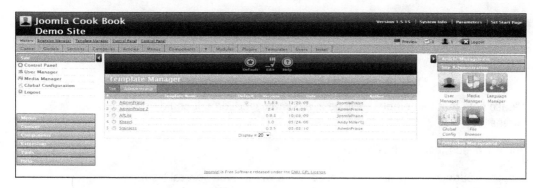

As you can see they are very different.

How it works...

Joomla! is built to have a method to separate the 'code' from the visual portions of the site. This gives you the ability to change the look for instance, by seasons if you are a online retailer, without ever having to rewrite your site's underlying code. The administrator template is exactly the same. Joomla! installs with a default administrator template, but the system allows you to install and set as default third-party administrator templates.

Screenshots for AdminPraise administrator template are courtesy of `AdminPraise.com` and `JoomlaPraise.com`.

There's more...

There are many template providers. However, for your convenience, here are three that provide administrator template replacements and skins:

1. `http://adminpraise.com/`
2. `http://www.joomlabamboo.com/`
3. `http://www.dioscouri.com/`

Manual installation of a template

In this recipe, you will manually uncompress (also known as unzip) the template which will contain several folders and files. Loading these up through FTP and then assigning in the Template Manager.

Getting ready

You will need to have acquired your template of choice for this step. There are quite a few resources for templates. Here are a few to get you started:

- `http://www.joomlashack.com/`
- `http://www.joomlart.com/`
- `http://www.compassdesigns.net/joomla-templates`
- `http://www.joomlapraise.com/`

Please note that the template will be in a compressed form. It could have a `.zip` or `.tgz` extension.

You will need the following items:

- Your new template compressed file (it will contain several files)
- Your FileZilla or other FTP client
- WinZip(R) or other compression utility

How to do it...

In this example we will be using WinZip to uncompress our file. If you are using any of the recent Windows operating systems, this will be built in. You can right-click the file to uncompress it.

Here is a summary of the steps necessary to install a template:

1. Using windows explorer (Right-click your **Start** button and click **Explore**).
2. Locate your compressed files.
3. Unzip it using WinZip or Windows compression.
4. Open FileZilla and connect to your server.
5. Open the `Templates` folder on your server.
6. Upload from your desktop the unzipped template to your `Templates` folder.
7. Once complete, login and go to **Template Manager**.
8. You'll see it and be able to assign it to your site.

   Here are the steps in detail.

9. Navigate on your desktop to the folder that contains your template file in its folder and right-click it. You will want to extract it to its own folder.

   This step will create a new folder that matches the name of the template.

10. Open your FileZilla client and connect to your server.

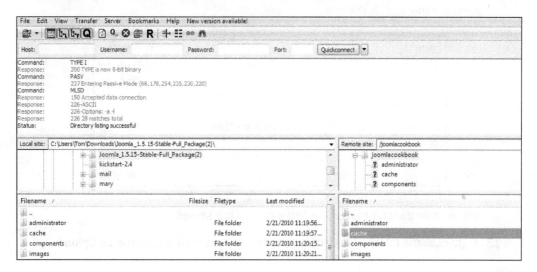

11. Navigate in the right-hand pane to your /templates folder and double-click it.

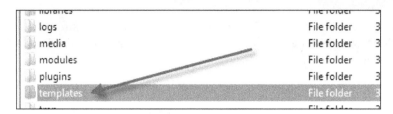

Here is how a default Joomla! template folder will look:

As you can see the default templates are located in here. For now we won't concern ourselves with those other templates.

12. In the left-hand window of your FileZilla client, navigate to where you have your UNZIPPED template folder.

    Here is mine:

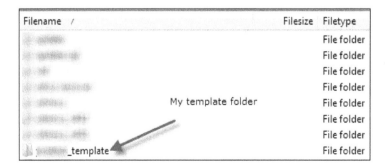

We will now transfer that entire folder over to our server.

13. Right-click the folder name and pull down the control panel, then click **Upload**.

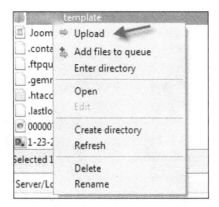

This will complete the transfer of the template over to the server. Be sure you FTP'ed or copied up the folder to the /template folder. For this example, we are using FileZilla and if you are, click the *F5* key to refresh your screen.

You should see an extra folder in your template directory now. Here is my server after the uploaded.

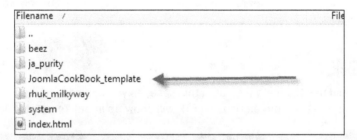

As seen in the preceding screenshot, we have a new folder. In this case, **JoomlaCookBook_template**.

Now we will verify it in the **Template Manager**.

14. On your main Joomla! Administrator Console, click **Extensions | Template Manager**.

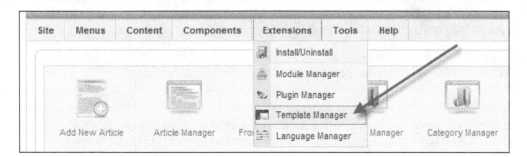

The **Template Manager** is where you will manage, assign, and edit templates. Once open, you should see the default templates and your new template. Here is mine.

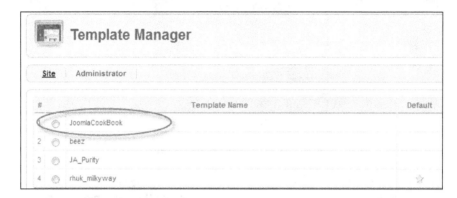

Default

The default template is the 'primary' choice for your Joomla! site. You may notice on the front end, that your site did not change. The "default" is set to **rhuk_milkyway**. Default templates are marked by a star. For now we'll leave it as it is.

How it works...

Normally you would use the installer, but in this case, as you can see, any valid template loaded into the /template directory using FTP will show up in our **Template Manager**.

Using more than one template on your site

In your Joomla! site you may wish to display more than one template to certain portions of your site. It's very simple to set up your site to display in this manner.

One reason you may wish to do this is if you have a different "look" you would want for your registered users, as opposed to the public users. This might be the case with the social community extension JomSocial (see Jomsocial.com). You might, in this case, use a template that has a style that may lend itself to encourages membership for your site.

Once the client or member joins, and they log in to your site, they could see a different "look" all together. This is easily accomplished by template assignments.

We will demonstrate this using the default **rhuk_milkyway** template that comes with Joomla! and the **JoomlaBamboo.com JB_ELEVATE2** template.

In this recipe we will assign different templates to various portions of our site. This particular recipe will have a few examples in it.

Getting ready

Your username and password for your administrative login.

(OPTIONAL) Follow the previous recipe for installation of a third-party template.

How to do it...

It is assumed you have already installed a third-party template, thus, we will skip over template installation. If you have not, please visit the previous recipe on how to install.

1. Open **Template Manager**.

2. Click **Template Manager** to open.

   This will display the available templates. You should see something similar to this screenshot:

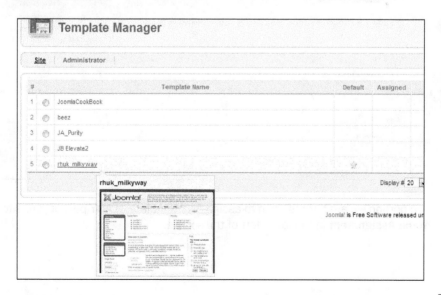

The preceding screenshot shows the thumbnail image of the default template for the site. Our instance of Joomla! has two additional templates installed. Your view may differ.

3. Choose your ALTERNATIVE template by clicking the TEMPLATE NAME.

Assigned and Default?

In our screenshot, you will see that the STAR is on the **rhuk_milky_way** template - this indicates that this template is the default for the site. Default for the site means that the assigned by default template that will come up first You may see the **Assigned** column has nothing in it. We'll cover that in this recipe, however, for a preview assigned it is checked when a portion of another template is assigned to a specific part of your site.

4. We will be choosing the **JB Elevate 2** template, as our alternative template for a few pages. Clicking on the template name shows this screen:

The portion we are interested in to assign ANY template to ANY part of your site, is **Menu Assignment** in the lower left of the screen:

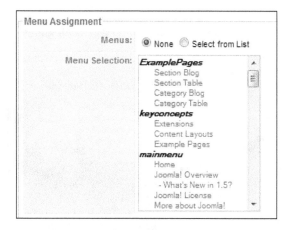

The current settings of **None** means that there is no assignment of this template to any portion of this Joomla! site. For our example, we want to assign the **JB Elevate 2** template to the **keyconcepts** section and categories.

To do so, we must first choose the radio button **Select from List**.

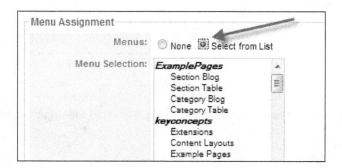

This will enable the **Menu Selection** portion that holds the sections and categories. Once done, we can select each category under the **keyconcepts** section.

5. To do so, hold down the *Ctrl* key while you select each one. In this example, I selected the **Extensions**, **Content Layouts**, **Example Pages** categories.

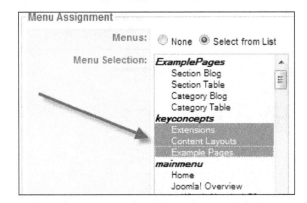

6. Once you make your selection then save your choice. Click **Save** in the upper right of the screen as follows:

7. Once you click **Save**, it will return you to the **Template Manager** window.

Apply

If you wanted to make other changes you can use **Apply** to 'apply the changes' but stay on the template screen

Now our **Template Manager** shows that we have a default, meaning that will be the first template we see when the site loads. And it shows an **Assigned**, meaning, we have assigned portions of the **JB Elevate 2** template to certain pages.

Template Name	Default	Assigned
JoomlaCookBook		
beez		
JA_Purity		
JB Elevate2		✓
rhuk_milkyway	☆	

8. Verify your work by clicking **Preview** in the upper right-hand corner of the screen. This will open a new window in your browser and display the front end of your site.

Let's look at a previous shot of the site.

Clicking **Extensions** on the left under **Key Concepts** (also known in this example as the left menu) would show this before the assignment of the **JB Elevate 2** template:

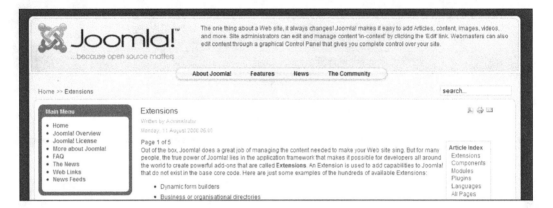

Now this is exactly the same content presented to the viewer when we assign the **JB Elevate 2** template to the **Key Concepts** section:

As you can see, there is a vast difference in the STYLE and LOOK, but if you follow this recipe, you'll see that the content remains the same.

How it works...

By assigning a default template, the system will render or display, your site based on that template. This is accomplished within the Joomla! code by inserting 'content' into a 'module' position. The template defines the module position, its style, fonts, colors, and so on. This allows a 'designer' to concentrate on style and the editor or copywriter to develop the content for the site.

See also

This particular recipe will be referred to again, however the reader may wish to see *Chapter 4*, *Editing Content and Menus* and *Chapter 7*, *Managing Articles Using the K2 Content Construction Kit* for further recipes related to this concept.

Determining your templates' module positions

Modules are built-in 'extensions' that are used to display your content to the website visitors. Using our example in the last recipe, you saw that you can make your site show a different template, based on the 'section' that is called. A module can be used in a similar fashion, showing components or other modules such as the **Login** module (also known as **mod_login**).

The module positions are placeholders, which are used to display content with the associated module.

Here is an example of the **Login** module being displayed in the left module position on the default Joomla! template **rhuk_milkyway**:

Login Form

Username

Password

Remember Me ☐

Login

- Forgot your password?
- Forgot your username?
- Create an account

The designer of a template has full control over module position locations and their names. You might recognize left, right, and banner. These are module positions available in the default Joomla! setup.

Module positions when left is right

LEFT, RIGHT, and other module positions are names only and do not always reflect the geographical position on the screen. Many times LEFT is on the left of the screen but not always. The developer has full discretion on their placement.

In this recipe we will look at the two methods to determine the module position for templates. The first one means using a command in the address bar of the browser, and the other method will be to use the **Template Manager** in Joomla! to determine the module positions.

This will be important as you design a site and want to place certain elements in specific locations.

Another tid-bit is many template clubs offer a variety of designs and they usually show the MODULE POSITIONS in a demo. Make sure that those modules exist in the production version of the template as well as the DEMO.

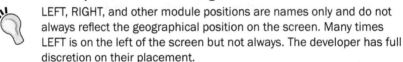

How to do it...

The quickest method to see a Joomla! site's Module Position is from the command line of the browser address bar. This works in most cases, however, there are some instances where it may not. In that case you need to have access to the template or to the administrator to determine its module positions.

Let's take a look at our demonstration site's module positions using the command line method.

▶ **Browser Command Line Method:**

1. Open your Internet browser and type this in, substituting your domain name where you see DOMAIN.COM.

   http://www.DOMAIN.COM/?tp=1

   This will provide you a view of the website with the module positions OVERLAYED onto the screen. Using the default **rhuk_milkyway** template we see this:

Zooming in a bit - you can see the names of the module positions overlayed in red.

The two module positions indicated are called **User3** and **User4**.

▶ **Administrator Console Method**

Occasionally there is a template that may not respond to that command or you may be working in the Administrator Console.

To view the module positions for any template from within the Administrator Console, follow these steps:

1. Login into your Administrator Console.

2. Open the **Extensions | Template Manager**.

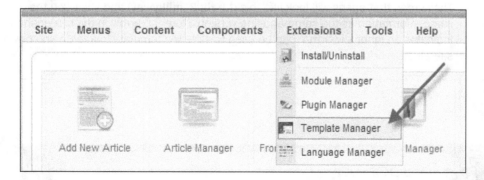

3. Click the radio button next to the template you wish to review the module positions for.

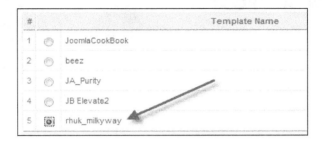

4. Then click **Edit** in the upper right hand portion of the screen:

This will open a menu devoted to the template.

5. In the upper right-hand side click the **Preview** button indicated by the arrow in the following screenshot:

The screen that opens will look like this (for **rhuk_milkyway**) and show you the same information as the command-line version. Note the arrow in the screenshot, it indicates an inner slider that can be used to slide the template image up and down to see all the module positions.

6. Once you are done reviewing module positions you may click the **Back** button and it will return you to the **Template Manager** or you may choose another destination from the top menu bar.

    Please note that using the **Back** button in your browser will give you a warning such as these:

    Firefox asks you to confirm:

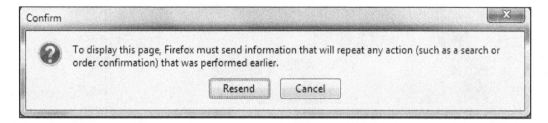

7. Simply click the **Resend** button (in case of Firefox) to continue.

    Internet Explorer 8 will give this scary-looking error - Click *F5* to continue through this:

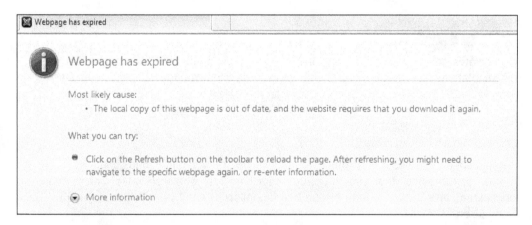

Internet Explorer 8 gives another version of the error, as shown in the following screenshot:

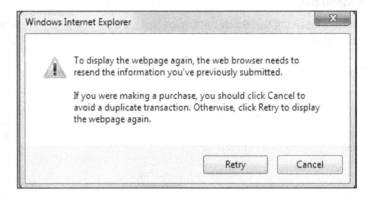

8. Click **Retry** and it will take you to the **Template Manager**.

   To avoid these errors, simply navigate elsewhere in your site by using the top menu bar.

How it works...

As templates are a form of an 'extension', calling the command from the browser, instructs this template to provide you a visual map for the extension. You may use the Administrator Console and see the same map of your template.

See also

The concept of modules is very important and will be discussed in various chapters, more in *Chapter 6, Managing Modules and Components*. For those who wish to learn more about the Joomla! template and framework please visit the following site:`http://docs.joomla.org/ Framework`

Replacing a logo in a template

Almost all commercial templates come with a default logo. While changing them involves artwork, replacing them is usually a simple matter of replacing the current image file that is represented in the template with one of your own.

A word of caution, you may be limited in size of the artwork the template will accept. I'll demonstrate replacing a logo on the **rhuk_milkyway** default template and the **BEEZ** default template.

Getting ready

You will need your "artwork" or new logo, your FileZilla client, and password.

To get ready let's use the **BEEZ** template, and identify what the LOGO file is called.

Our first template logo change will be on the **BEEZ** template. For this, I already assigned the template to our site and it looks like this:

Now to see the "logo" of this particular template, right-click **BEEZ** in the upper left of the screen. You should see this:

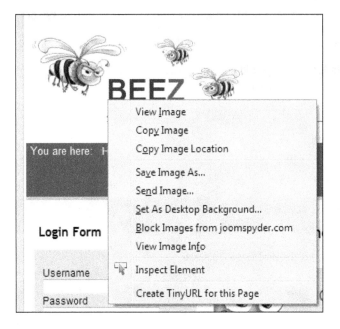

Click **View Image** and you will see:

This reveals our 'logo' in this template. We can see the name in the browser bar, as shown in the following screenshot:

http://www. /joomlacookbook/templates/beez/images/logo.gif

In this case the logo is identified for us as `logo.gif`, in the `templates/beez/images/ folder` on our web server. We are now ready to replace it with our own logo.

How to do it...

1. Open FileZilla **Site Manager** and log in to your web server.

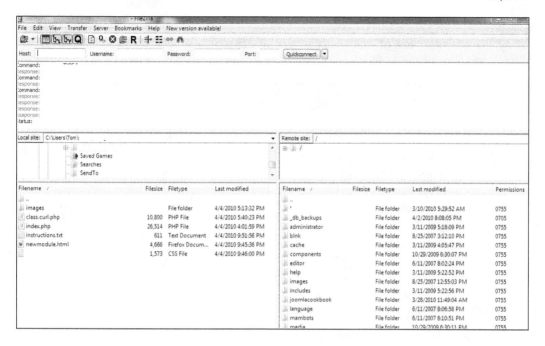

2. Navigate to `templates/beez/images/`.

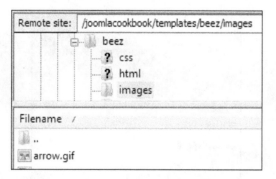

3. Scroll down till you can locate the file `logo.gif`.

Our next step is to preserve this original file and upload our new `logo.gif` file.

4. Rename `logo.gif` to `old_logo.gif`.

   In the right pane of your FileZilla client, locate the `logo.gif` file and right-click to rename it to `old_logo.gif`.

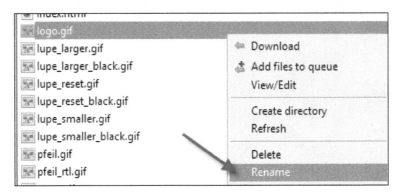

5. Upload new `logo.gif`.

   In my example, I created a new logo and saved it as `newlogo.gif`.

   Open FileZilla (if not already open).

   Locate your new logo in the left panel of FileZilla and click it to highlight and select **Upload**:

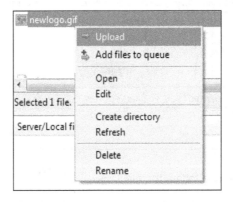

6. Rename your logo to `logo.gif`.

   Following the previous instruction for renaming, in the right panel, locate and rename `newlogo.gif` to `logo.gif`.

7. Adjust size in code

   Go up one level by clicking the **...** in the file list. You should be at `yourdomain/templates/beez`. Locate the file `index.php`.

8. Right-click the file to edit it.

You will now be in the `CODE` section of `index.php` - we need to adjust the 'size' of the graphics. Currently, the default **BEEZ** template is set for the following:

300 x 97. This matches the current BEEZ logo. Our new logo is much larger so we need to adjust for it.

9. Scroll down to line 44 and at the end of the file you'll see this:

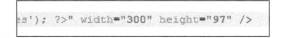

Our new logo is 550 x 120 - so we'll change the width and height to match and save the file and save it back to the site. You should be aware that you will need to replace the image with the one that will fit within this template's dimensions. Otherwise, you'll experience problems in the layout. As a suggestion, if you do not care about the template layout, locate one that has a more fluid design. Or one that can accommodate your graphics. For a detailed look at Joomla! 1.5 templates, you may wish to purchase Packt's *Joomla! 1.5 Template Design* book.

10. Now visit your site and you'll see our new logo:

How it works...

This logo, like most templates, is easily replaced. In this example, the logo required an adjustment in the `index.php` file of the template.

Joomla! reads this file and adjusts the template to fit the logo in question.

4
Editing Content and Menus

In this chapter, we will cover:

- ▸ Installing a new editor
- ▸ Setting up sections
- ▸ Setting up categories
- ▸ Article creation
- ▸ Adding new menus
- ▸ Setting up a blog on your Joomla! site
- ▸ Adding an extension menu

Introduction

Websites exist to communicate information to their intended audience. Using a content management system such as Joomla!, makes managing the content even easier.

Joomla! gives you the ability to add content to our sites and manage it. By attaching the content to menus we have a great means for our audience to interact with and consume our content.

You will learn how to set up the basics of a SECTION and a CATEGORY to hold and manage content.

Menus are important and Joomla! can have as many menus or as few as you want. The trick is to use menus in a manner that makes sense for your site and follows prescribed best practices for usability. An example may be you want your visitors to purchase your goods or services. In that event, you would not want to bury your "BUY NOW" button behind three menus. Make it easy for them to do business with you.

Installing a new editor

An editor is a miniature word-processing application that is built into Joomla!. It gives you a simple means to edit your content and apply formatting.

Joomla! comes with a default editor called TinyMCE. The **TinyMCE editor** is a good starter editor and provides basic colors, formatting, and a few other essentials.

One area that can trip you up is writing a beautiful article in Word, cutting, and pasting it into the editor and it looks horrible on site. TinyMCE has the ability to 'paste' into it using a WORD import function. However, there are many other editors which offer better features.

There are some commercially available editors that offer a higher level of word-processing type support, making it even easier to manage your articles and content.

Replacing the default editor in your Joomla! site with the JCE editor will give you a more powerful editor to manage your content. This recipe will show you how to download, install, and assign the editor.

Getting ready

To start this you will, of course, need your Joomla! Administrator password. We will need to download the editor from the source. Once you have the password you are ready to get started.

The default editor that ships with Joomla! is called TinyMCE. Following is a screenshot of the TinyMCE interface:

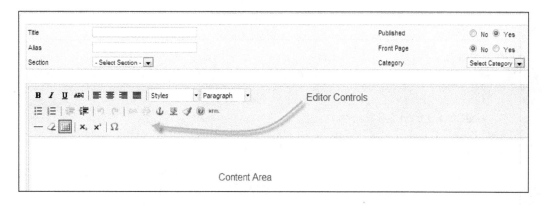

As you can see there are very limited controls. After you install the JCE editor you will see a completely different view.

How to do it...

The steps to complete these are:

1. Download JCE from `http://www.joomlacontenteditor.net/`.
2. Log in into the Administrator Console on your site.
3. Upload and install the editor.
4. Assign the editor in the Global Configurations.
5. Download JCE.

    You will need to open your browser and point it at `http://www.joomlacontenteditor.net/`.

6. Browse to **Downloads**.

7. Choose **Editor** for **Joomla!1.5.x**.

8. The next screen you see will be the selection screen:

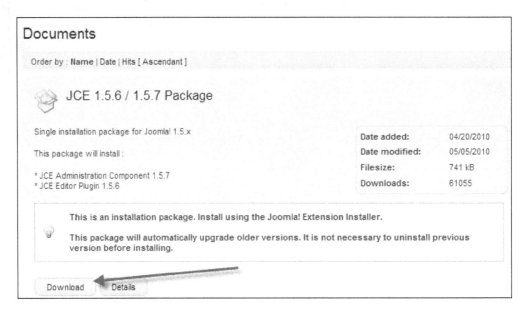

9. Go ahead and choose **Download**. Don't forget to note where you downloaded it.

10. Log in to your Administrator Console in your Joomla! site.

11. Log in to admin and navigate to the installation screen:

12. Choose **Install/Uninstall**.

    Next browse for the JCE extension:

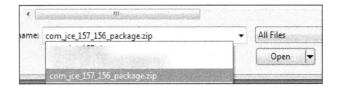

13. Select the package name, in this case it's **com_jce_157_156_package.zip**.

    The version number may vary by the time you read this. If so the file name will be different.

14. Click **Open**.

    This will start the installation process and once it completes you'll see this screenshot.

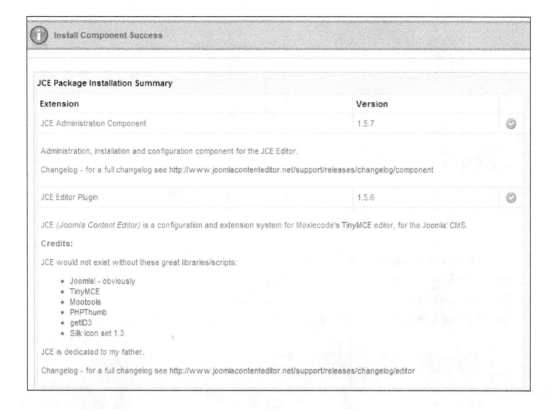

    The next steps will be to assign this as the default editor.

15. Assign JCE Editor to your site as the GLOBAL editor for all users.

    While still in your super user admin console navigate to **Global Configuration** as follows:

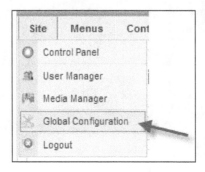

16. Click **Global Configuration.** You should be at this screen:

17. Pull down the **Editor - JCE 1.5.6** and click **Save**. This will assign it as the DEFAULT editor to your site.

18. Test.

19. Click the **Content | Article Manager** on the top menu bar as follows:

We'll start a new article solely to look at the power of the editor.

20. Click the **New** button in the upper right-hand side as follows:

This will open a blank article. Remember the image of TinyMCE? Here is your new editor screen:

As you can see there are many more options - giving you greater control over the content.

How it works...

You have now assigned the 'editor' function of your site to this particular task; it will be the editor of choice until changed or replaced.

You can override it on a per user basis, but there is usually no need to.

This editor which is now set for GLOBAL, will be applied to all users who edit content on your Joomla! site. You can override this on a per person basis if you wish.

 There are many commercially available editors that can be implemented in your Joomla! site as well. Have a look at http://extensions.joomla.org for more.

Setting up sections

Sections are the topmost portion of your Joomla! site. They are the guidepost to the rest of the content in your site. In this chapter, we will go through the process of setting up a section.

Getting ready

There are many schools of thoughts for sections. You can imagine a **section** is like a filing cabinet drawer. It holds many file and folders. **Categories** are like the files and folders in the cabinet drawer. Within a file folder, we have papers and other media, such as photos, or cd-roms, or other things. Sections are the containers that hold categories. A section can have many categories. Articles, like the metaphorical paper, is content and its tied to a category. So the order is **Sections | Categories | Articles**.

You have the ability to define sections any way you like based on how you want to order your content. I would suggest that you use sections for major portions of your site. Examples can include NEWS, PRODUCTS, HELP, or SUPPORT. It really all depends on how you divide up the content on your site. Use categories to break down sections into something that makes sense to your audience. The Products section could contain two categories; Free and Paid, or Hardware and Software.

Adding articles at that point is simply a matter of placing it in the right section and category.

To get ready, we should determine what our section will be. In this case, we're going to need a Product News - Widget-Widget World section about our Widget Products.

In the section just created, we'll have many categories such as product news, services, financial and so on. We can create articles for those.

Determine what you want for your first section; get logged in to your Joomla! Administration Console and let's get started.

How to do it...

1. Open the menu **Content** and select **Section Manager**.

This will take you to the following screen:

2. In the preceding screenshot, there are sections already in place. In this example, we have **About Joomla!**, **News**, and **FAQs**. These were installed using the **Sample Data** button at the time the Joomla! installation was completed.

3. While still in the **Section Manager** click **New**.

You'll be taken to this screen:

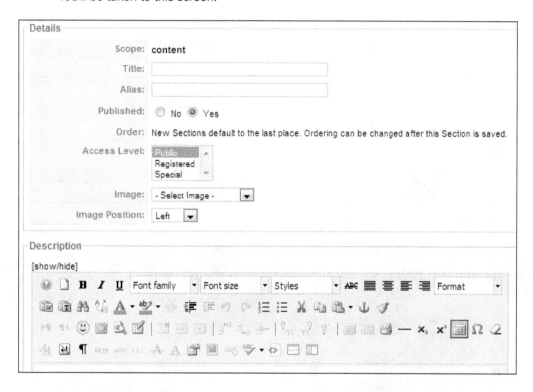

4. Fill in the **Title** - keep in mind this is viewable so it should make sense.

5. Fill in the **Alias** - This is internal for you – for example, products from `widgetworld.com` - additionally, this can be used for search engine friendly URLS.

6. Select your **Access Level** (default is **Public**)

7. **Image**: This can be any image you want - logos, brand, anything that you have. The images are stored within the `Images` folder and referenced in the database.

8. **Image Position**: Default is **Left** - for our example we're going to leave it left.

9. In the **Description** area, fill in the details (optional).

    Here's our example all filled in.

10. Now click **Save** and you are done - you will see the following:

Your new **section** is ready to use.

How it works...

We have 3 major sections as shown in the following screenshot, **About Joomla!**, **News**, and **FAQs**. They are indicated by the header **Title**.

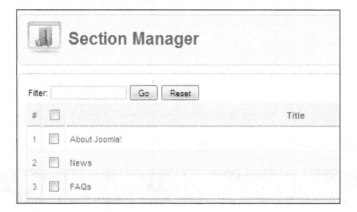

Moving to the right, we see:

▶ **Published**: Indicating it is available for use

▶ **Order**: (Which order the sections appear in)

▶ **Access Level**: In this case **Public** means that the SECTION is publicly available

Continuing to the right, we see the next parameters **-Select State-** which allow us to filter. It is *VERY useful if you have a LOT of sections*.

▶ **#Categories**: This lists the number of categories in that section.

▶ **#Active**: The number of active articles within this section or category. This will include all published and unpublished articles but will not count those in the trash bin.

▶ **#Trash**: Self explanatory.

▸ **ID**: Joomla! automatically assigns this number for internal use. The ID coincides with the database information. Additionally, with some extensions such as Dynamic Header Images, you will reference this number.

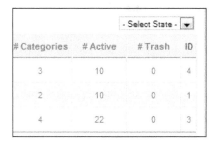

	- Select State - ▾

# Categories	# Active	# Trash	ID
3	10	0	4
2	10	0	1
4	22	0	3

This completes our setup of our sections. Next, will see categories to live in those sections.

Setting up categories

In the hierarchy of content, Sections are first and they contain categories. Categories contain articles. In this recipe, we will follow up on sections and learn how to set up a category.

Getting ready

We can really get granular in terms of content management with categories. What you will need is one or more categories that you will file your articles in. You'll need to have the section that this category belongs in already created.

We will be adding categories to our Section **Product News-Widget World**.

If you are not the Joomla! Administrator, go ahead, log in, and let's get started.

How to do it...

1. Choose **Content | Category Manager**.

2. The following screenshot shows the full screen of Category Manager. Let's look at each section in detail.

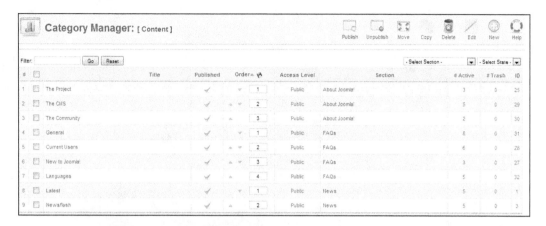

3. The left-most part of the screen, labeled as **Title**, is the categories we have set up. These, by the way, are installed by Joomla! when you install your sample data. Once you create one you'll see it in your version of this screen.

4. Moving right, we have several items here.

Published	Order⌂		Access Level	Section
✓	▽	1	Public	About Joomla!
✓	⌂ ▽	2	Public	About Joomla!
✓	⌂	3	Public	About Joomla!
✓	▽	1	Public	FAQs
✓	⌂ ▽	2	Public	FAQs
✓	⌂ ▽	3	Public	FAQs
✓	⌂	4	Public	FAQs
✓	▽	1	Public	News
✓	⌂	2	Public	News

- ❑ **Published**: Yes/No - if not checked (red x) this category won't display
- ❑ **Order**: In what order do you wish them to appear in
- ❑ **Access Level**: Options are **Public** (anyone can see), **Registered** (only those registered can see), **Special** (admins only)
- ❑ **Section**: What section this category belongs too

[Note that in the last section, we see that MANY categories can belong to ONE section.]

5. All the way to the right we see these three parameters.
   - ❑ **# Active**: How many articles are active in that category
   - ❑ **#Trash**: Self explanatory
   - ❑ **# ID**: This entry, like the afore mentioned, SECTION ID, coincides to the database reference and will be critical to you in some situations.

# Active	# Trash	ID
3	0	25
5	0	29
2	0	30
8	0	31
6	0	28
3	0	27
5	0	32
5	0	1
5	0	3

6.   Click **New**.

This starts the process of setting up a new category.

There are several substeps involved in category setup.

- ❑   **Title**: This is the title of your category
- ❑   **Alias**: Internal for your use - won't be displayed
- ❑   **Published** or not
- ❑   **Section** (choose one)
- ❑   **Access Level** (select appropriate level)

▸   **Public** is essentially anyone browsing the site. They do not have access to login or make any changes

▸   **Registered** are the categories of users who have been granted the rights to login to the site

▸ **Special** is the administrative user only

❑ **Image** (optional) and **Image position**

❑ **Description**: What is the category about

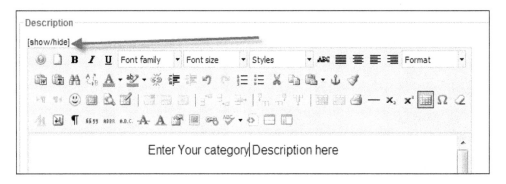

7. Select **Save**.

How it works...

Let's go ahead and add a category to our section Product News - with our first category being WidgetWorld.

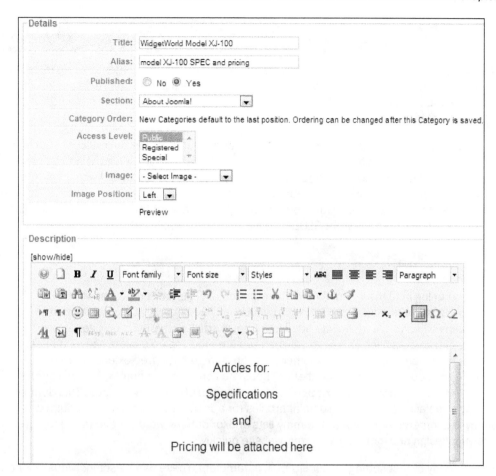

Here we have completed our WidgetWorld software specifications category. I put it in the Product News-WidgetWorld section.

Again, play with the categories and get very comfortable with them and make sure that they are exactly as you need them. If not, it's easy to delete a category and recreate it.

Your new category is ready for use.

Article creation

Articles, also known as content, are really the heart of your Joomla! content management system. They are the reason Joomla! exists. In this recipe we'll create an article and assign it a category and section. This will help you as your site grows, and you create more content and make it available.

As you proceed through this, you'll note that many of the settings reference Global. Within Joomla!, you can set specific parameters *Globally*. That is to say, providing them to all articles the same way. If for instance I ALWAYS want to show the Title in an article, I would set that globally, and simply leave the global setting as is for each article. If I had a specific article that I did not wish to display the Title for I could change that locally for that article only. Changing the title setting in the article from GLOBAL to NO, would accomplish this.

Getting ready

You'll need to log in to the Joomla! Administrator Console. For our purposes, we will be generating content to put it in an article from `http://www.lipsum.com/-` you can do the same while you learn how to build and format articles. `LipSum.com` generates Lorem Ipsum 'text' as filler. This is great when you are mocking up a client site, and need to put text in before it's available. Another great tip is to grab the free extension from `opensourcesupportdesk.com` that will populate Lorem Ipsum dummy text in a site. `http://www.opensourcesupportdesk.com/extensions/downloads`. This dummy text Plugin replaces a tag within Joomla! articles (or a Joomla! Custom HTML-module) with dummy text, ordered or unordered dummy lists and/or dummy words. It allows you to develop, prototype, design and/or test text in your website quickly.

Let's get ready by first setting all our GLOBAL parameters. These can be set individually for an article anytime, thus overriding the global settings.

- ▶ Log in to the **Super Administrator** article
- ▶ Locate **Parameters** in the upper right-hand side of the screen and click it
- ▶ This will show you all the global parameters for articles and allow you to set them
- ▶ Once complete, hit **Save**

This will now be the default for new articles. Changing individual article parameters is simple and fast.

How to do it...

1. From within **Administrator**, choose **Content | Article Manager**.

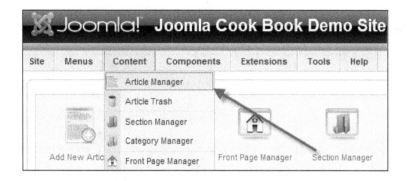

Or you may also choose **Article Manager**, located on the main administration page, to see a full list of your articles.

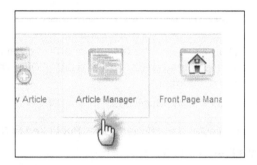

Once in, you see this screen which contains the controls to manage articles as well as a list of published and unpublished articles.

2. Click **New** to start a new article.

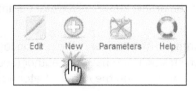

You can also select the **New Article** button from the main administrator control panel and reach this screen.

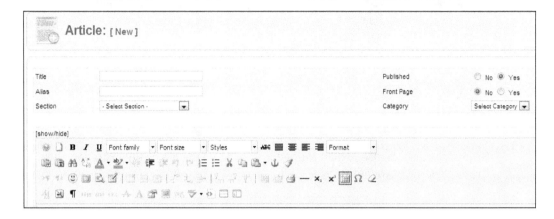

Once you are there, you can begin the process of article creation. You will need to give it a title, an alias and assign it to a SECTION and CATEGORY. The alias, if left blank, will be auto-generated by Joomla!.

Remember **Title** is what the world will see.

3. As we do not wish to display this article yet, set **Published** to **No**.

4. The next portion is **Front Page No/Yes**.

   This one you will want to pay particular attention to. If you select **Yes**, your article will display on the home page. That may or may not be where you want it.

   For now - we'll leave it **No**.

5. The right-hand side of the article shows us several parameters. The first is **Parameters (Article)**

   You can see in this example - the **Author** is the person logged in. In this case, I am logged in as the Administrator. If you have the author (see next screenshot) selected to be displayed, in the articles, then the Administrator would be listed as the person who wrote it.

In my example, I want this to be someone else in the title.

6. **Author Alias** will show whatever I want on the **Title** of the article, enabling me to put a name or a title.

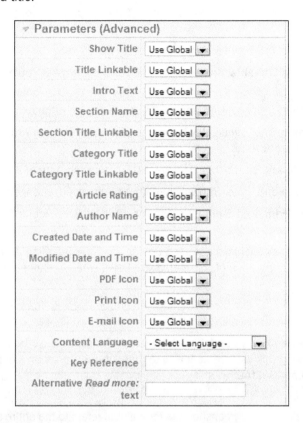

As discussed at the beginning of this recipe, the global settings will apply to your article. Thus, if you haven't set them in **Article Manager | Parameters**, you will see the defaults. You can however change them at any time and it will immediately apply to all current and future articles.

The Parameters right below the previous are the Advanced parameters. These can be set per article as you see here.

7. You see the default here is **Use Global** - or use the setting set Globally.

8. **Show Title**: This tells Joomla! whether or not to display the Title of the article in a heading tag (default is **Use Global**).

9. **Title Linkable**: This will enable the title to reach a full copy of an article. If you have a long article, you will want to use READ MORE. Clicking the Title (if enabled) will take you to that full article.

10. **Intro Text**: Think of this as a snippet, or teaser. It will only show a small amount of the full article when the article is first displayed.

11. **Section Name**: Tells the system to show (or not) the section name.

12. **Section Title Linkable**: Same function as **Title Linkable**, except links to a section page.

13. **Category Title**: Displays (or not) the category title.

14. **Category Title Linkable**: If you enable this, clicking it takes you to the category page itself.

15. **Article Rating**: This allows (if enabled) viewers to RANK the article.

16. **Authors Name**: This will display the name of the person who wrote the article, and works with **Author Alias**.

17. **Created Date and Time**: This displays INITIAL creation date of the article.

18. **Modified Date and Time**: Shows when it was last saved/changed.

19. **Icons - PDF**, **Print**, and **E-mail**: Enables or disables these icons/functions from the displayed article.

20. **Content Language**: This is not used unless you have installed optional language packs into your instance of Joomla!. If you have, you can choose the language of your choice here.

21. **Key Reference**: For our purposes, this will not be used. To learn more about it see: `http://forum.joomla.org/viewtopic.php?f=394&t=34676`.

22. **Alternative Read more text**: The default is READ MORE... at the article break. However, using this you are at liberty to make it unique. As an example READ MORE... could become "Get the full story".

In the previous screenshot, the term global refers to the entire scope of the site. In other words, if you apply a article setting globally, each article will use that setting.

This is handy in many situations and as you see in Joomla! 1.5, the concept of a Global setting takes on even more importance.

23. In this screen, you fill out the items that are important to search engines such as the **Description** of the page, **Keywords** of the page. The ROBOTS issues `robot.txt` type commands to the search engine such as "index" or "Index, follow (other links)".

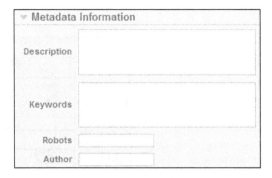

24. Fill in our real information. As you can see in the following screenshot, I have filled in my **Title**, **Alias**, and so forth.

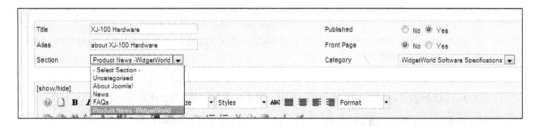

As you can see the article is filled out, but not formatted. In the next step, we'll format it a bit to make it presentable.

25. Use formatting tools.

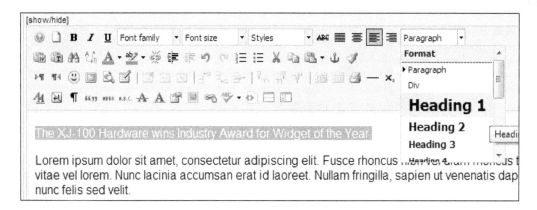

In this step, we'll use the formatting tools to make the text more readable. To call attention to the areas we want to highlight, let us start by adding **H1** to the title, and **H2** to the intro text as follows:

The result is a nicely formatted article, shown as follows. The title is on, and the article header is set in **H1** font, with the first paragraph set for **H2**.

XJ-100 Hardware

XJ-100 Hardware wins Industry Award for Widget of the Year.

Lorem ipsum dolor sit amet, consectetur adipiscing elit. Fusce rhoncus nibh vel diam rhoncus tempus. Aliquam at nisi a dui venenatis laoreet vitae vel lorem. Nunc lacinia accumsan erat id laoreet. Nullam fringilla, sapien ut venenatis dapibus, nunc risus vestibulum libero, at elementum nunc felis sed velit.

Pellentesque quis massa dui. Nullam aliquet, massa nec commodo laoreet, quam dui accumsan urna, id ullamcorper magna magna quis eros. Duis nibh velit, tempor eget commodo condimentum,

26. Change the parameters.

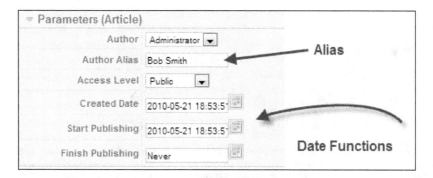

27. Add an **Author Alias**, if you are logged in as admin - otherwise your articles will be shown as created by **Administrator**.

28. Set the **Created Date** to either the current date or your preferred date.

29. Set the **Start Publishing** date. This enables you to prepare content ahead of time and have it auto-published.

30. **Finish Publishing** will remove it at that day and time.

31. Fill out metadata for the search engines.

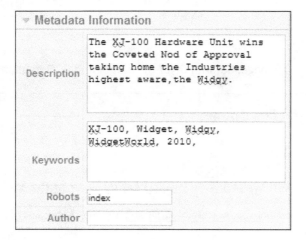

Here is the completed article, with email, PDF, print, and author information turned on.

Here is the same page, but with ONLY the author and PDF creation icon turned on.

More Info Section 1

It has been mentioned many times earlier about 'READ MORE'. The following section shows you how to actually use it.

Open the article, and position the cursor where you would like the READ MORE to be positioned. Click the ---- button as you see in the following screenshot (**article.readmore**)

Once done - you'll see the grey bar underneath the cursor position. This tells the article generator to break this article up.

This is a great feature for articles that scroll on and on. You can provide a small amount of text and allow the reader to move into the article if they like.

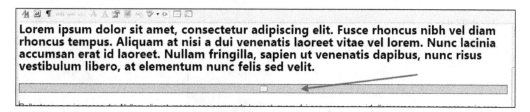

Here is the same article with the **READ MORE...** link in it. Clicking that would yield the full article.

Adding new menus

To help your visitors to navigate your site, you'll need menus. The menus in Joomla! can serve multiple purposes. Adding menus for articles and for extensions is a simple process in Joomla!. In this recipe, we'll look at how to add new menus.

Getting ready

In a site you were planning on putting into production, you would want to map out the menus on paper, determine what content goes where, and so forth. In this example, we'll go through a basic menu setup, along with a couple of examples.

All you will need to do at this point is to login to your Administrator Console.

How to do it...

1. Log in.
2. Choose **Menus | Menu Manager**.

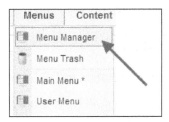

You will see a list of your menus and the parameters of each.

3. Next click the **New** menu button.

4. You will see the new menu screen as follows:

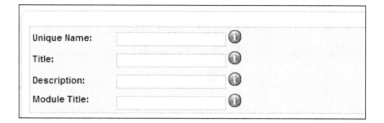

5. Now fill in each of the fields and click **Save**.

How it works...

Now that we have seen the basic steps, let's go through the example (starting with the last preceding step)

Before we add our new menu - you see the menus listed as shown in the following screenshot:

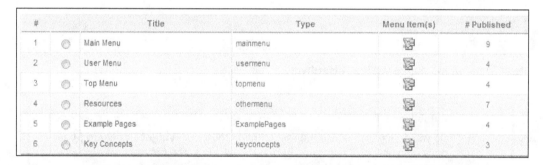

#		Title	Type	Menu Item(s)	# Published
1	⊙	Main Menu	mainmenu		9
2	⊙	User Menu	usermenu		4
3	⊙	Top Menu	topmenu		4
4	⊙	Resources	othermenu		7
5	⊙	Example Pages	ExamplePages		4
6	⊙	Key Concepts	keyconcepts		3

Now we will repeat the previous step and add our new menu item.

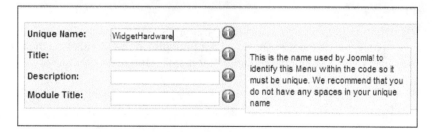

 As you can see the dialog box in this screenshot is open telling us a bit about the importance of this particular field.

We added the **Unique Name** as **WidgetHardware**, now we'll add the other fields in this screen.

We have completed it - now click **Save** and you'll see it show up as follows:

#		Title	Type	Menu Item(s)	# Published
1	⊙	Main Menu	mainmenu		9
2	⊙	User Menu	usermenu		4
3	⊙	Top Menu	topmenu		4
4	⊙	Resources	othermenu		7
5	⊙	Example Pages	ExamplePages		4
6	⊙	Key Concepts	keyconcepts		3
7	⊙	Widget Hardware Spec	widgethardware		-

Item 7 now shows our new **Widget Hardware Spec**.

Published

Do you notice that unlike the rest of the menus, our **Widget Hardware Spec** does not show ANY published items. This is due to the fact that we have not 'assigned' anything TO that menu yet. We'll do that in a later section.

There's more...

Creating a menu item will cause it to show up as a "module" in the Modules section of the site. Let's look and see the state immediately after creating the menu item.

menus - post widget creation

You see our 'menu' is called by its UNIQUE name of **widgetspec**. Further, it is not published. We will need to publish, set the access level, and so forth before we can use it.

Assigning an article to our new menu

When you return back to the main control screen for admin., you should see this:

▶ Choose **Menus | Widget Hardware Spec**.

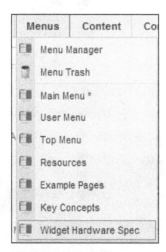

▶ You are now in the menu itself for **Widget Hardware Spec**. Here you can add, change, or delete menu items. Additionally you can do many other tasks that will be covered shortly.

This shows us - that we do not have anything in yet. We're going to add an article to this menu item.

▸ Click **New** to add a new menu item.

This will open up this large screen - filled with options - we'll consider the **Articles** portion first.

▸ Select **Articles**.

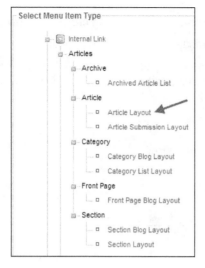

▸ We will choose **Article Layout** for this example.

▸ In this step, we will add the article, and set all the various parameters.

 Take your time in this section as there is a lot of information.

Zooming in on the left hand-side of the screen shows us the following:

- ▶ **Title**: This will be the publicly displayed name of the menu item - such as Specifications.

- ▶ **Alias**: This is the internal name - you can choose whatever makes sense for you.

- ▶ **Link**: This is automatically filled in for you by Joomla!

- ▶ **Display in**: This shows you where this item will be displayed. In other words, what menu you want this article to be attached to. If we were to pull down the drop-down menu, we would see:

- ▶ **Parent Item**: This is a hierarchal listing - you can use this for submenus. We'll leave it as a TOP item for now.

- ▶ **Published** defaults to **Yes**: However, you can unpublish if you are not ready for the world to see it.

- ▶ **Access Level**: This defines the access level or permission level the users must have to see it.

- ▶ **On Click, Open In**: This gives the target browser instructions on what to do when this menu is chosen.

Access Levels

- ▶ **Public**: Everyone can see this item

- ▶ **Registered**: You must be a registered user of the site to see or use this resource

- ▶ **Special**: Only the logged in administrative users of the system can access this.

  Continuing on with the other controls, we move to the right- hand side of the screen:

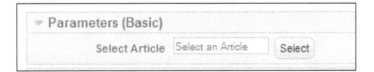

This is an extremely important control for this particular article. Here, we attach the CONTENT (in this case the article) to the menu item.

▸ Now click **Select**.

▸ We will scroll down now to the article of your choice:

▸ Click the article of your choice. This will fill in the parameters into the article for you.

▸ The next column below is **Parameters**. There are several choices you could make here. As each article and website will be different, your choices will also vary.

We want our clients to send the WidgetWorld information to all their friends, be able to print the specifications sheet, and create a PDF. Let us take a quick look at those.

If our "GLOBAL" setting was set to **Show**, then we could have left it as **Use Global**, However we want to make sure that no matter what, this page has these turned on. Thus we have set them to **Show**.

This will create the following on the page when displayed to our viewers:

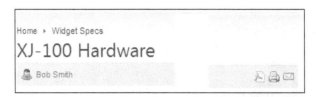

Once you have changed any other items of interest, you can click **Save**. You'll now see the article on the front page. Here's our example:

Setting up a blog on your Joomla! site

Given that Joomla! is a content management system, it's perfect for managing a blog. In this recipe, we'll go through the steps of setting up a 'blog' on your Joomla! site.

How to do it...

I have added two articles to my website. These will form the basis of adding that content as a blog.

My first two blog articles are:

 ▸ Day 1 at the Widget Factory
 ▸ A tour of widget engineering

We can set up several different types of blogs on Joomla!, each has a connection back to the way that you have set up either section or category. Additional options include setting them in various layouts.

We'll look at each one, starting with the category blog.

1. Log in.

2. **Menus | Main Menu**.

 You can pick any Menu you wish - for simplicity I have chosen the **Main Menu**.

3. Open the **Main Menu** and select **New**.

   You should see this:

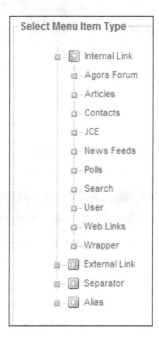

```
Select Menu Item Type
         Internal Link
           Agora Forum
           Articles
           Contacts
           JCE
           News Feeds
           Polls
           Search
           User
           Web Links
           Wrapper
         External Link
         Separator
         Alias
```

4. From here, open **Articles** and you'll see this:

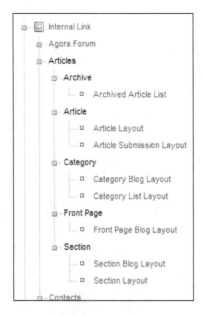

5. This is where you will select the type of blog you want. We're starting with the **Category | Category Blog Layout**.

6. Select **Category Blog Layout**.

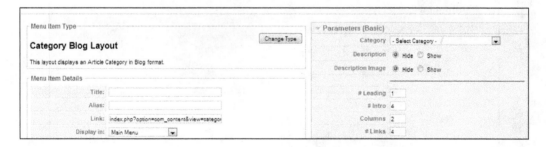

This partial screenshot shows the most important parts we need to deal with. Let's look at the left side first:

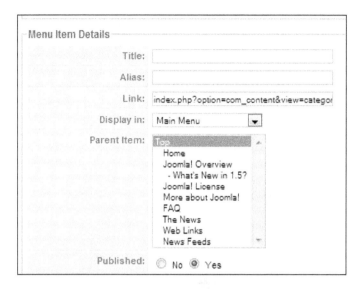

This left portion is where we will name our "blog" and the alias. The parent item allows us to position it where we want to. An example may be a submenu.

Let us look at the right hand of the screen now:

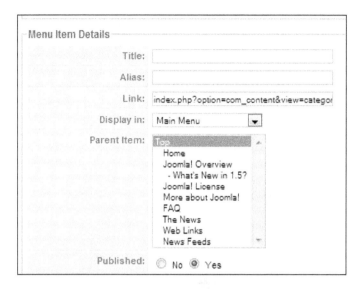

Here is where we select the **Category** of the articles we want to blog about. As we have set up the category previously, we're ready to go. The next step will be to fill those in.

7. Choose the category you want.

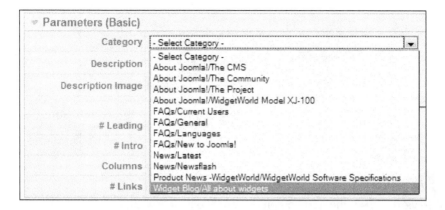

8. Here we have pulled down, the Category drop-down menu and have selected the **Widget Blog/All about widgets**.

    As this is a blog, we don't want to overwhelm people with a thousand articles about our topics. Rather we give them a few articles, and then links.

9. Set blog article parameters.

    In this step, you will establish how you want the blog to appear. I will set mine in the manner I wish to and show you. In the "How it works" section, I'll explain about the parameters.

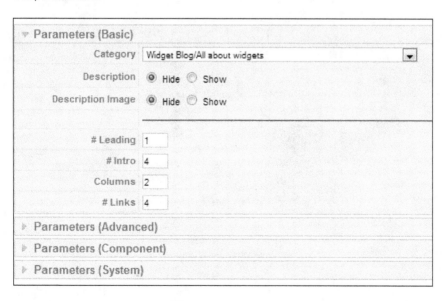

I have set mine as follows. This will format my blog accordingly.

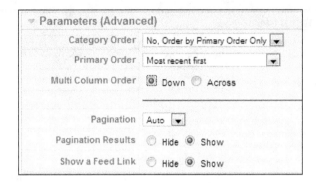

10. Review and set the next screen on your site as follows:

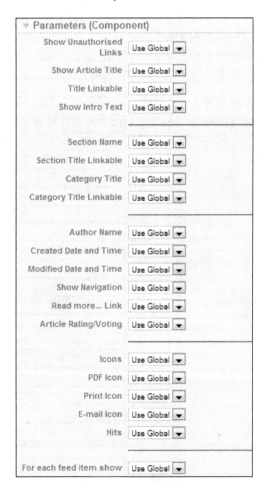

11. Click to the next panel **Parameters (System)** and set the parameters accordingly:

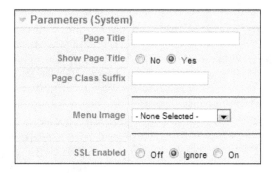

In this we will leave everything as default.

12. Now that everything is set - we have a final step, that is, to PUBLISH our blog.

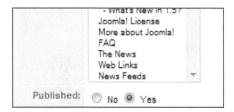

13. Click **Save** and we are done. Here's my blog on the first page of my website.

Here are my two blog entries complete with **READ MORE...**. If I had several entries, you would see below four of the most recent links to the articles. That parameter is set in the **Category Blog Layout | Parameters (Basic)** -- # links (4 in my case)

14. This following screenshot shows a formatted blog entry:

How it works...

The 'blog' is simply a way to organize content in a chronological fashion. This differs somewhat from publishing an article to your home page. By publishing our content to the blog format, you can keep a running diary of information that your site visitors would find handy.

Let's look again at the parameters and see how they can enhance your blog.

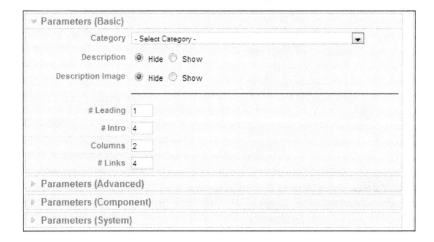

- ▶ **Category**: We selected a category blog for this example. In **-Select Category-** you would choose the category that represents the articles you wish to blog about.

- ▶ **Description**: This is a description that you put into the CATEGORY setup of the blog.

- ▶ **Description Image**: If you have a company logo, or other pictures for your blog you may wish to show it here - this is either **Hide** or **Show**. It pulls this from the Category image.

  The next four are very important to how your blog looks and is used.

- ▶ **# Leading**: This is the leading blog entry number. In our case, as you can see, I have set it to **1** .That means one article across the COLUMN. Default is 2 - thus 2 articles. You may wish to set this to zero if you want a full width across.

- ▶ **#Intro**: This displays the number of blog articles that show up with their titles, the introductory text (before the **READ MORE...**). In case of my examples, I have two articles in the blog, but if I had 4, then all four would be seen on my blog page.

- ▶ **Columns**: This means - how many columns do you wish to display across - in this event 2, but it is meaningless because I set leading to **1**. If you set this leading to **1**, then you should set **Columns** to **1**.

- ▶ **# Links**: If you are a frequent blogger, you will have many articles that start to show up. This setting will show the number of PREVIOUS blog entries in the form of a LINK. This enables the reader to quickly find the last few.

  I suggest you leave this at its default of 4 for readability, but your site will dictate its needs.

  There are many methods to set up and divide your blog content. Play around with the various settings and find out what works best for your layout and content.

Adding an extension menu

Extensions are add-on applications that extend and enhance the Joomla! framework. They add all kinds of functions from simple calendar applications all the way to the ones with rich features such as the Agora forum.

In this recipe, we'll learn how to get the Agora forum to the menu on our home page for Widget Aficionado's to meet online and talk.

Getting ready

Before you can assign this extension, you must install it. Joomla! 1.5 has a universal installer, which means most 'extensions' install via this means. It is noteworthy, that some extensions are not handled in this manner, but that is beyond the scope of this book. For our purposes, plugins, extensions, components, and even templates are all handled with one installer.

To handle this, we'll need to install Agora first. Please visit `http://www.jvitals.com` to download the extension.

Installation is done in a few simple steps.

If you aren't already logged, then do so now.

▶ Once you have logged in, navigate to and select from this screen:

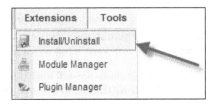

▶ Selecting the installer will start up the sequence and allow you to install.

▶ Choose your extension and click **Upload file & Install**. In this screenshot, I have selected the Agora extension.

Once done you'll get a message as follows:

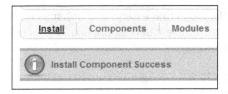

Now that the extension is installed we are ready to assign it to a menu.

How to do it...

With our new Agora Forum (from `jvitals.com`) installed, we will:

Create a new menu for it.

1. Assign it into that menu.
2. Activate and view from the front end.

   Let's begin by creating our new menu.

3. Select **Menu Manager**.

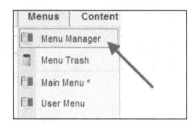

4. Select **New** menu and fill in the parameters. Here's my example:

5. At your end, you will need to fill in the particulars of your menu. Be sure and click **Save** when done.

   We have filled out the parameters and now we have a 'menu' in which we can load Agora.

6. Click **Save** and you'll see your new menu. Here is mine.

 There are no entries in the right column for **Widget World Forum** - that is because we have not assigned anything to it yet.

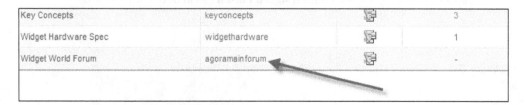

Key Concepts	keyconcepts		3
Widget Hardware Spec	widgethardware		1
Widget World Forum	agoramainforum		-

7. We will now add the Agora component to our menu. Choose **Menu | Widget World Forum**.

The next screen that opens will enable us to actually set the **Agora Forum** component to a menu item.

As you can see the menu is currently empty.

8. Click **New** in the upper right-hand corner of your screen.

You'll notice in my screen I have a **Agora Forum** as an option for a menu.

9. Select the **Agora Forum** option.

Menu Item Type

Change Type

Agora

One of the most eagerly awaited releases for Joomla, Agora 3.0 Olympus is finally here! The jVitals team has been working vigorously on this project in an attempt to make it the best possible Joomla component available. Imagine, No bridges, No hacks, just the finest fully integrated Forum Component solution for the Joomla CMS available.

Built from the ground up to be robust and efficient, Agora 3.0 has a large feature set which can not be ignored. There are also many add-ons which will be made available immediately for use with Agora, such as integrated modules and plugins.

Agora 3 is the future of integrated forums. It includes all the features that you expect from an advanced Forum, such as; Quick Post, Ranks, Awards, Image & File Attachments, Advanced Searching, Announcements, Subscriptions, Polls etc... Agora 3.0 also includes many features you will not find elsewhere, such as;

- Enhanced Warning and Banning system
- Enhanced User Group system
- Enhanced User Rolls
- Built in Private Messaging
- Translated into 31 different languages
- More...

All of this, plus optional integration with Community Builder, JomSocial and Joomunity and support that is second to none! Visit the jVitals website for more details.

We see the preceding screenshot for the top half and below it are our settings.

10. Now fill in the details in the following screenshot:

11. The next step is OPTIONAL - and is only shown here for completeness SSL (encrypted sessions) for Agora.

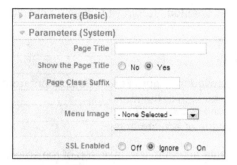

For our needs, we aren't handling sensitive information, so we'll leave it in **Ignore** mode. However, turning the **SSL Enabled** radio button **On** would force Agora to serve up its data using a secure session.

Using a secure session

In order to use a secure session on your Joomla! site, you will need to purchase a SSL certificate from your host. They will need to install it on the server. Most webhosts offer these at a reasonable annual cost.

12. Activate **Module Menu**.

13. Click **Extensions | Module Manager** as follows:

You'll see, by default that the menu for Agora is actually a module, and is disabled by default.

14. Click the red **x** under **Enabled** - turning it to a green check. Now it is ready for use.

How it works...

In the previous steps, we installed the Agora Forum Component from JVitals.com, created a menu, and assigned the extension to the menu.

Now we'll want to make a couple of adjustments.

By default, a new menu module automatically is on top of the stack. Thus, any menu module you create will be on the very top.

We don't want our Main Forum or **Widget Spec** above our **MAIN MENU**.

▶ Open your **Menu Manager** again and locate the **AGORA MAIN FORUM**:

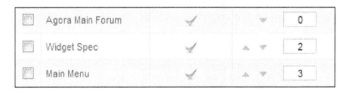

The **Agora Main Forum**, **Widget Spec**, and **Main Menu** are listed as 0, 2 and 3. We want them to be:

▶ **Main Menu: 1**

▶ **Agora Main Forum**: 2

▶ **Widget Spec**: 3

To bring about this change, either use the up and down arrows or you may renumber them accordingly:

- Once you have the order set, it's important to save it .Click the Floppy Disk icon as you see in the following screenshot:

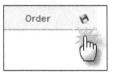

- Click the Floppy Disk / Save icon on the top bar.

  Now we can look at the front of the site and see the menus are in the order we wish them to be:

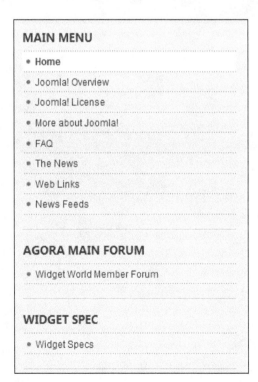

▶ Clicking on our new **Agora Main Forum** link - **Widget World Member Forum**, will take us to the Agora Forum.

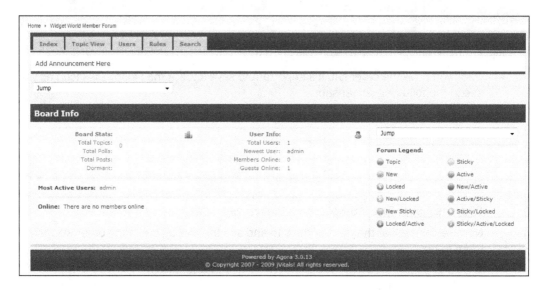

5
Managing Links, Users, and Media

In this chapter, we will cover:

- ▸ Adding a new user
- ▸ Deleting a user
- ▸ Suspending a user
- ▸ Assigning a user to a group
- ▸ Using contact manager
- ▸ Managing login and user experience
- ▸ Uploading media
- ▸ Creating a folder in media manager
- ▸ Using web link manager
- ▸ Changing lost super admin password

Introduction

Management of the elements that make up your site is an important task that you as a site owner or administrator should be well versed in.

If you have a heavily trafficked site, with a lot of users joining, you might spend a decent portion of your time managing users. In other scenarios, you might have a site with no registered users, and thus, you might spend little time in the USER MANAGER.

In this chapter we'll take a look at managing links, users and media - a broad brushstroke of all the elements.

Let's get started.

Managing users

A normal but often over looked task is the management of users from your website. This can result in leaving users in who shouldn't be there. Other times, a user needs their details updated and so forth.

This recipe will guide you through several tasks related to the management of users.

Getting ready

You will need your Super Administrator login, and a couple of sample users to experiment with. We'll start with ADDING a user first that way you can build up a couple of samples for the rest.

You will also need to come up with names, email addresses, and passwords for them.

How to do it...

1. Login into your Administrator Console. That is www.YOURDOMAIN.com/ administrator.

2. Open **User Manager**.

You'll be taken into a list of your users and the actions that you can take for each. In this case, we'll need to create a new user.

3. Click **New** to create a new user.

4. The left side of the screen is where we'll start.

- ❏ In this screen, fill in the **Name** (proper first and last name) of the user.
- ❏ Choose a unique **username** which is also known as the screen name.
- ❏ Fill in **E-mail**. This is necessary to send the user the login information.
- ❏ Choose a STRONG password and repeat it in the **Verify Password** column.
- ❏ Select **Group**. In this example, choose **Registered**.

The default state of the two radio buttons is both **No** - leave them as is for now.

5. Parameters.

- ❏ Setting these parameters by user is optional.
- ❏ **Back-end Language** (I chose **English (United Kingdom)**): Pick the right one for your needs.

- ❑ **Front-end Language**: Pick the right one for your needs.

- ❑ **User Editor**: In our case, we have the **Editor - JCE 1.5.6** as the default one. If you have not added a new editor, you likely will see TINYMCE.

- ❑ **Help Site**: This defaults to help.`joomla.org` - leave it there for now.

- ❑ **Time Zone**: This is the time zone for the user. In our case, it is Hawaii time.

6. Here is an example filled out.

7. Save your work

- ❑ That completes the creation of a user.

How it works...

The previous process creates a profile for the user, and puts them into the database. As part of that creation process, the users' preferences are stored. This enables you to set up specific profiles by user.

When they log in, they will get all their specific settings.

Disabling user accounts

When a user no longer needs their account, a good practice is to disable them. This way they can be reactivated.

1. Login to your Super Administrator account.
2. Choose **User Manager** icon.

3. From your list of users, pick the account you wish to disable.

4. Choose the user by clicking their name.
5. Scroll down till you see this screen:

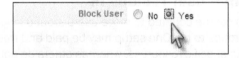

6. Select the **Yes** radio button - and click **Save**.

    With this set to **Yes**, the user will not be able to login. This sets a field in the database that blocks the user.

    Additionally, they won't be able to register again with this email because the email address is still in the system.

Deleting a user

Occasionally, a user will need to be deleted. This is a very fast process.

1. Log in into the Administrator Console and, again, select **User Manager**.
2. Once you have chosen your user, check the box as follows:

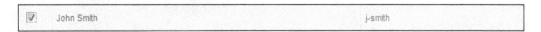

3. Next look up in the upper right of the **User Manager** screen:

4. Click **Delete** and this will remove the user from your site and your database.

CAUTION

This is a permanent operation - once you delete the user is gone. You'll need to rebuild them or recover from a backup, in case you delete them by mistake.

Once you successfully delete the user you'll simply see them leave the database.

In Joomla! 1.5, it does not give any messages warning you or letting you know that you have deleted a user.

Changing the group a user resides in

There are more ways than can be counted to move users around in groups. And it all boils down to what YOU need groups to do. One setup may be paid and free groups. Another might be users who get access to specific resources, whereas others do not.

That is really up to you and your needs. However - we handle them all the same way.

Let's take our example user - William who is currently a "registered" user. That means he simply has an account on our site.

William is now going to be part of our team and take care of some of the administrative tasks on the site.

1. Opening the **User Manager** in the administrator, and finding William's account shows us his group:

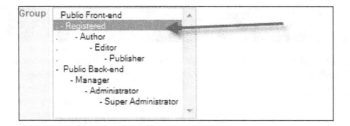

William now needs to be an administrator, in our next step we'll move him there.

Why not Super Administrator?

The Super Administrator account has full rights to the system and can do anything they want. It's a very good practice to restrict use and access to the Super User account. You should create an administrator account for your own use for daily operation, leaving the Super Administrator ONLY for when you need it. In case of William, he's a third-party doing work for us, so we'll want to make sure we grant him the LEAST privileges he needs to get his job done.

2. Still in Williams account that is open, click **Administrator** as follows:

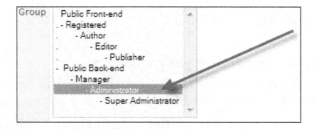

3. We must now **Save** this.

William is now an administrator and can log in to the backend, create users, and other administrator tasks.

Setting up a site contact

Joomla! has the ability to manage contacts for your visitors. Joomla! gives you multiple ways to engage your site visitors with this. Some areas that might be of value to you are say, setting up separate contacts for support or sales.

In most sites, there is the ability for your visitors to reach you via your site. This is typically a section called CONTACT US. Joomla! has the native ability to make this easy to do through the use of a CONTACT FORM. The SITE contact is the means to do that.

The beauty of this is that it hides your email address from the public, thus lowering the chances a spam bot will grab it and add you to its list.

If you have to change a contact name, you can simply change the name and contact information and Joomla! handles the rest. Now when someone sends you a mail through the site, their note is routed to you based on the email listed in your contact.

Getting ready

You'll need to have the contact information for someone to populate the fields.

How to do it...

Setting a default contact on your website

Every site typically has a 'contact us' section. Joomla! makes it simple for you to assign one or many contacts to your site as the contact person.

Let's carry on from the last recipe, and make William our contact person for the site. Before we set the default user, here is the message you'll see for accounts NOT assigned to CONTACTS.

```
Contact Information

No Contact details linked to this User:
See Components ⇒Contact⇒ Manage Contacts for details.
```

As you can see the user does not have any contact information set up for them. This is the default for ALL users.

We need to set up William for various tasks.

1. Logged in as administrator, click **Components | Contacts** and then **Manage Contacts**.

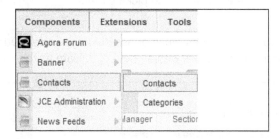

As we don't have ANYONE set up as a contact then we'll see this:

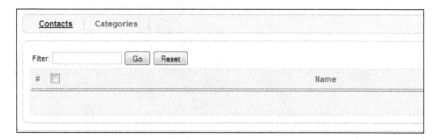

You see the entire selection is empty.

2. Select **New** in the upper-right corner. This will take you to a screen with a lot of fields. This is the new contact section:

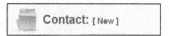

3. Add in all the necessary details. Note that there are several screenshots for this page.

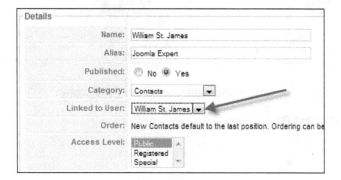

In the DETAIL section, you'll need to FILL OUT the name and alias. It defaults to published, and public.

4. Pull down the **Category** drop-down menu and choose **Contacts**. Then choose the user by selecting **Linked to User** and picking them.

Personal Information.

In this screen you can input as much or as little as you need. Our screenshot is completely filled out - complete with a photo of William as the contact image.

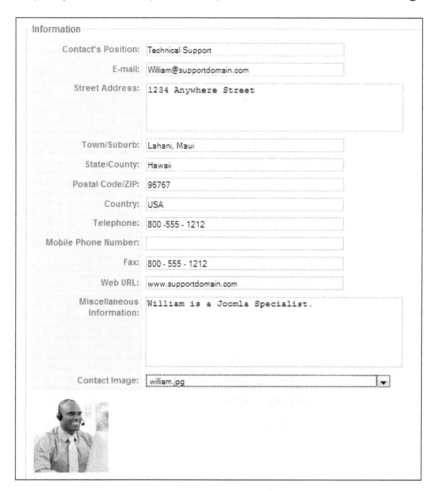

Our next step is located on the right hand-side of the screen.

5. Setting **Contact Parameters**.

These **Contact Parameters** will vary by site. In our case, we have set them as follows. You may see that we have hidden the **E-mail** and **vCard**. Hiding the e-mail, keeps down SPAM to a certain degree.

6. **Advanced Parameters**.

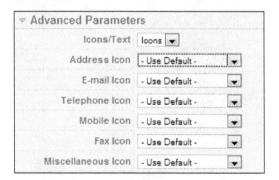

The advanced parameters are primarily graphics. Choose them according to your site style. I find that the default Joomla! parameters work quite nicely.

7. **E-mail Parameters**.

This will enable or disable the Contact Form. The other items on the screen such as **Banned E-mail**, **Banned Subject**, and **Banned Text** exist to reject e-mail that has these words, or addresses in it. A typical use might be profanity, or to known harassing e-mail addresses. While not fool proof it offers a measure of protection.

We said that William was set up and ready to receive calls, but we have an additional set of steps we have to accomplish.

We need to create a MENU item for the contact.

Let's go through that now.

Setting up a contact menu item.

How it works...

Joomla! will look in the user table and fill out the appropriate contact information based on what you put in the contact sections.

This again is a terrific way to segment contact by department, functions, locations, or many other ways.

As with all things in Joomla!, there are several extensions available that offer greater functionality than the basic contact form.

Spend some time defining your needs, and then see what the Joomla! Extensions directory has to offer.

By installing a third-party extension on the site that offers features that enhance your contact page you will give your site a very polished look and feel.

Working with media

Media is a big part of a Joomla! site. This can include music, animation, pictures, and more.

Joomla! has a very powerful media manager built in it, which enables you to categorize and assign all types of media.

Getting ready

You'll need at least one `.jpg` or `.png` image to work with.

To get started, log in to your Administrator Console.

How to do it...

1. Open **Media Manager**.

Once open, the Media Manager has several items of interest:

We're going to add some advertising images to the **banners** folder.

2. Click on the **banners** folder icon (see the preceding screenshot).

We are now positioned in the folder we wish to upload a file to.

3. Scroll to the bottom of the screen till you see **Upload File** control. Please note this is available at all times in the **Media Manager**.

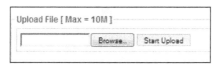

4. Click on **Browse...** and find the file you wish to upload. This will be browsing your local machine.

5. Once you locate it - click **Start Upload**.

You'll note that there is a new image in the line-up of banners now.

We chose **banners** specifically for this example to install additional advertisements to display on our site.

How it works...

Media Manager is just a giant file manager. It reads the structure that Joomla! sets up, or, that you set up during the course of your site's life.

One specific folder is the **banners** folder. The banner management code looks for pictures to display in the banner module position. It's wise to think about how you set up the media manager in relation to what you want to accomplish.

Segmenting your media, perhaps by client or subject, helps you keep it fresh and current.

There's more...

Media Manager offers an explorer-type menu system that allows you to view the images in your image folder.

You can add as many folders as you need and then use media manager to add, change, or delete content from within them.

Navigating the media manager tree

There are two ways to navigate through the media folders.

The simplest way is to choose the folder you wish to open. In this example, the arrows are pointing towards the M_Images and the stories folder - these are both default Joomla! folders.

You could open any of these by clicking the `Folders` icon.

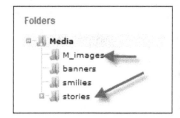

The second method is to choose a folder from the **Thumbnail View**:

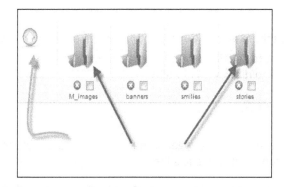

Here we can accomplish the same thing by clicking on any of these folders.

Do you see the bent arrow on the left? It is pointing to the up arrow which will take you one level up in the directory. This view is called the **Thumbnail View**.

We can alternate between **Thumbnail View** and **Detail View** quite easily:

- Clicking on **Detail View** changes our view to one that's more "DOS" or list-like:

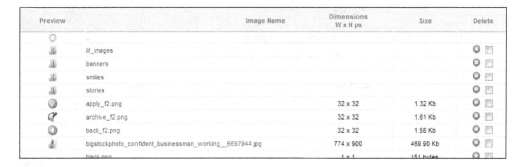

Preview	Image Name	Dimensions W x H px	Size	Delete
	..			
	M_images			
	banners			
	smilies			
	stories			
	apply_f2.png	32 x 32	1.32 Kb	
	archive_f2.png	32 x 32	1.61 Kb	
	back_f2.png	32 x 32	1.58 Kb	
	bigstockphoto_confident_businessman_working__6697944.jpg	774 x 900	469.90 Kb	
	black.png	1 x 1	151 bytes	

One great advantage to the **Detail View** is it gives us **Dimensions W x H px** (in pixels) and image size.

Why is the image size important?

The size of the image can greatly impact your site's performance. If an image is too large, then the visitors will have to wait longer for the site to load. This can cause them to move on if they are impatient.

A good resource to check for what's bogging down your site's performance is a tool called: http://pingdom.com/ - it will show you by image (and other resources) how long each takes to load.

Creating a folder

There are many times you need to create a folder. In this example, we need a widgetimages folder.

▶ While still in Media Manager, type in the folder name and click **Create Folder**:

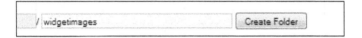

We're creating a **widgetimages** folder.

▶ After clicking **Create Folder**, I see the following:

Now I can store my widget images in the widgetimages folder.

Deleting an image or a folder

If we left images on our server that we no longer need, it will make it harder and harder to keep track of what we DO use and what we DO NOT use.

Deleting is easy. Returning to the **Media Manager**, we're going to delete a file OUT OF the widgetimages subdirectory.

▸ Click into the `widgetimages` directory - and in our case, we have a single image.

▸ Click the red **x** of the item you wish to delete. This will immediately delete it.

The image is now deleted.

What if you want to delete more than one image at a time? Mass deletions can be done by selecting all the files you wish to delete by checking them as follows, and clicking **Delete** in the upper-right corner.

Let's say we're done with our directory as well. We cannot delete it UNTIL it's empty - which we accomplished in the previous step.

▸ Click the green arrow to go back up by one level.

Find your directory you wish to delete. In this case, we need to delete the
`widgetimages` folder. Click the red circle **x** and the folder will disappear.

A word of caution

Make sure that the media you are deleting IS NOT in use. If you do - the
article or extension that depends on it will not work properly.

If you attempt to delete a folder that has media content in it, you'll see this error message:

I attempted to delete the `M_images` folder. It cannot be deleted as long as images are in it.

Managing the login and user experience

The login is the portal for your users to reach your content that is meant exclusively
for the subscriber.

There are many things you can do with the login to enhance the customer experience.

In this recipe we'll look at the Login Module, how to redirect after login and logout and how to
modify it for a better customer experience.

In the first part of this, let's examine how we can use the Login Module to communicate to our
clients-literally giving them a set of directions on how we wish them to interact.

Getting ready

- ▶ Login to your Administrator Console.
- ▶ Navigate to **Extensions | Module Manager**.

- ▶ You will need to locate your login module. It should be labeled `mod_login` under the type column.

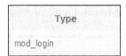

- ▶ Click on the module to open it. You should see this:

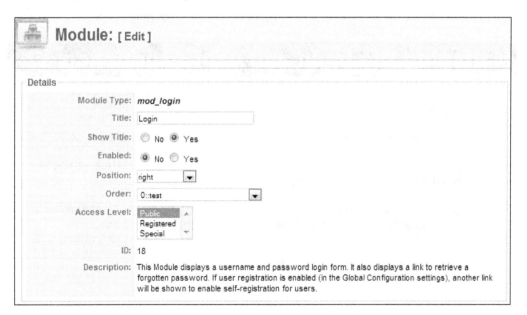

In this image, we have the Login Module opened for editing. Here you can change the **Title**, manage its position on the screen, and publish. If you not wish to display the **Title**, you can select **No** at the show title option.

How to do it...

As you can see in the previous screenshot, the default **Title** is **Login**. Let's look in detail at each one of the major sections of the Login Module. We'll end up with this as our login:

For WidgetWorld, we are interested in communicating the legal aspects of using the login (authorized to use ONLY for registered users), as well as all the contact information needed.

1. Our first change will be the **Title** - from **Login** to **Widget World User Login**.

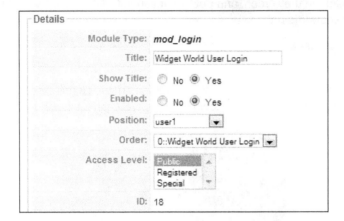

There are several changes we made from default.

- ❏ **Title: Widget World User Login**
- ❏ **Show Title: Yes**
- ❏ **Enabled: Yes**

This gives us a Title on the Login Module as well as making sure it is useable. For our template, we have it in **user1** position - yours will vary.

2. Next we'll assign the pages, we want this login to show. For our site, we want it on every page, as follows:

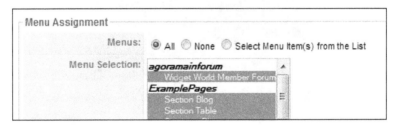

3. Next we'll set up the main features we saw earlier:

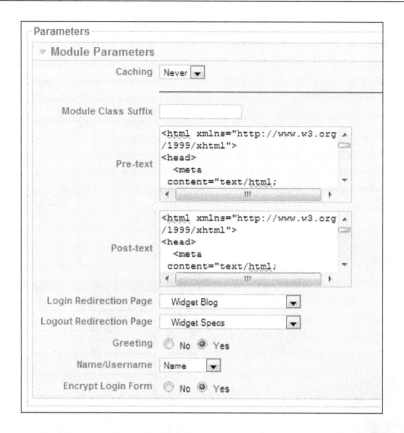

- In the **Pre-text** you can have normal text or you can use HTML. We chose HTML to give us the ability to style it the way we want. **Pre-text** is shown at the top of the module.

- The same applies to **Post-text**.

- **Login Redirection Page**: In our example we want the registered users to land on the Widget BLOG page. This is where we'll communicate information to them like product news, industry updates, and more. So - when they log in they are taken directly to that page. You can do the same with any page on your site.

- **Logout Redirection Page**: When they sign out, we want to once again have their attention on our WIDGETS. After all for us, it's about reaching our clients and keeping their focus on purchasing more widgets. Upon log out they will be directed to a Specifications Page.

▶ **Greeting**: This is either **Yes** or **No**. If you greet them, you have a choice in the next box, of using their Name (from the user manager) or their login name.

▶ **Encrypt Login Form**: You may choose **Yes** or **No**. We have chosen **Yes**, because we are very concerned about security.

In order to use the Encrypted Login Form or SSL, you'll need to have a properly installed SSL certificate. This is a purchase and most of the time the HOST has to install on the server. SSL certificates add a great deal of privacy for the person browsing. The session between the user and the server is encrypted with SSL. This prevents a malicious person from reading what you're doing. SSL is required in any type of e-commerce, banking, and in other instances where privacy of the information is paramount.

4. If you're happy, click **Save**.

When our users' log into the site they'll see something like this:

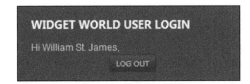

How it works...

The Login Module is essentially an 'extension' like any other ones. This one, however, ships standard with Joomla!.

The Login Module reads, the user's credentials from the database, and if valid, will grant them access to the resources.

The login can be disabled, thus preventing ANYONE from logging in from the front side.

Additionally, you can login as an administrative user from the front as well.

There's more...

Quite a few developers have produced improved or more feature-rich Login modules for Joomla!

They are easy to install and usually work just well too.

Let's go through an example:

Changing to a third-party login module

1. Login to your Administrative Console.

2. Go to **Extensions | Install/Uninstall**.

3. Locate your extension and upload as follows:

4. In this example, we obtained a module from the Joomla! extensions directory (Joomla.org). You can substitute any module you wish if you do not want to use the Login Module replacement.

5. Now we'll upload the third-party `mod_signallogin.zip` - click **Upload File & Install**.

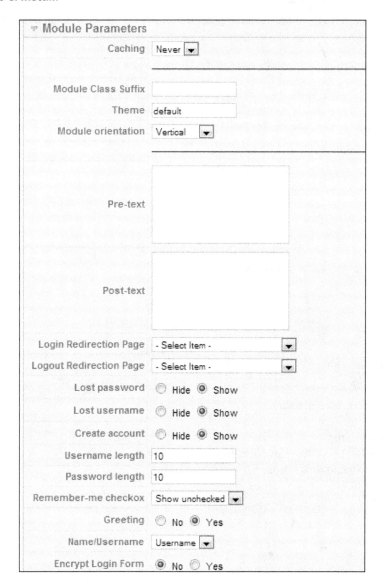

The left side of this extension is identical to the default Login Module. Let's focus on the enhancements.

▸ Different "Themes" to display.

▸ You can set the direction vertically or horizontally.

▸ You can enable or disable or change:

    ❑ Lost username or password

    ❑ Create user

    ❑ Set maximum lengths for username and password

    ❑ Remember ME checkbox

You can see a HUGE difference there. This is one of the MANY logins that can be added. We have one other change to make

▸ Navigate to **Extensions | Modules** and locate your new Login Module. Once there, it should be disabled by default. - Enable it.

▸ Click the red **x** to enable.

▸ Next find the normal **mod_login** - it will be enabled – disable it:

▸ Click the green check to disable.

What you have just done is replaced the current stock login with another one. By disabling the stock login, and enabling the new one your users will be directed over to it.

A search on the `http://extensions.joomla.org` site will reveal many different types of Login extensions.

Web Link manager

The Internet itself could be thought of as a collection of 'links', as in sites that list other sites. Many times these are favorites, for more information, and so on.

The Web Link manager allows you to collect and categorize all your favorite links for your viewers and get them on your site.

In this recipe we'll go through the basic steps to setup the necessary category and links.

Getting ready

For your site, you'll need to choose one or more links that you would like to display. Additionally, you need to determine a category for them.

In our example, we want to have a category called Development. In this we'll list several Joomla! resources.

How to do it...

1. Open the Administrator Console

2. Navigate to **Components** | **Web Links** | **Categories**.

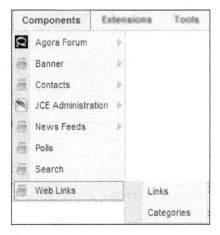

3. Click **New** in the upper right-hand side and you'll see the **Category** screen:

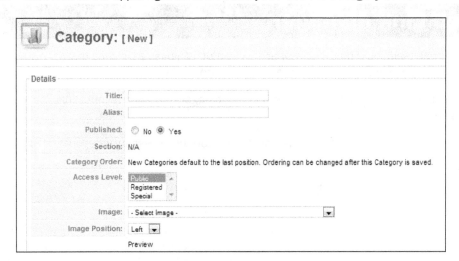

4. Fill in all the information relevant to your topic. Here's a copy of mine:

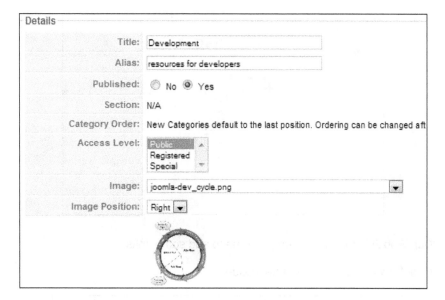

5. In the box below it - **Description**-you can fill in the appropriate description.

6. Click **Save**.

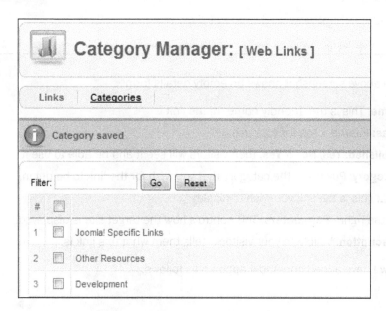

There in our Web Links you see item 3 is our new "category".

Now that we have our category set up, we'll need to add links:

7. Open the **Components | Web Links | Links**:

Our 'WebLink' manager is empty. Time to add some links

8. Click **New** in the upper right-hand side.

The above screenshot shows an empty details form.

▶ **Name**: This is the "friendly name" of the link

▶ **Alias**: Internal alias for your use

▶ **Published**: **Yes/No** - if **Yes**, then visitors will see it and be able to use it

▶ **Category**: Pull down the category that you wish for the link to be put in.

▶ **URL**: This is the link you wish to display.

▶ On the right - **Parameters**: This controls how the target site is displayed.

▶ **Description**: Visible to your visitors - tells them what this link is.

9. Now I have added one and it appears as follows.

I have filled in a few more and now my Web Links page looks as follows:

From here, I can add, change, or delete my links.

How it works...

The "Web Link" component has a special place in a Joomla! site. It is a very easy–to-use mini-database of your favorite links for your visitors.

In the following screenshot, I clicked **Web Links**:

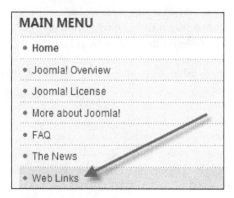

I then clicked through my category called **Development**, and then I am presented with the links that are specific to **Development**.

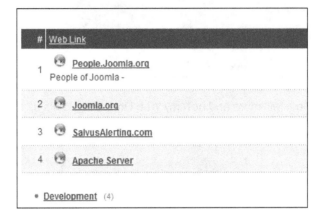

This is a handy way to categorize links and make it SIMPLE for your visitors to find the information they need. This is also a neat way to gain some search engine visibility.

Changing lost super admin password

It happens for a variety of reasons but people lose their Super Administrator passwords. This can be a very bad thing, if you cannot retrieve it. In this recipe we will see a sure fire method to quickly change the password and gain back control of your site. There are a few situations where this might be the case, such as someone changing the e-mail and password without your knowledge. Or in another instance, hackers have attacked the site. Lastly, if you have inherited a site to manage and do not have access to the e-mail.

One means of getting a super user password is to request it through the forgotten password mechanism. However, that only works if the Login Module is on and you can click the forgotten password. For sites without a front-end login, you must have the password to gain access.

Normally, if none of this applies, you can simply request it as stated above, from the front-end of the site.

Getting ready

To accomplish this, you'll need to do the following:

▶ Determine new password

```
http://www.tooljo.com/joomla-15-password-hash-generator
```

▶ Visit this site and create a new 'hash' by putting in your password, calculating hash, and copying the resulting HASH.

- Get your cPanel phpMyadmin password (or equivalent means to get to the database).
- A new e-mail address for your Super Administrator (optional if the password on file is not yours).

How to do it...

You will need to log into your cPanel or other control panel to reach your **phpMyadmin** screen to manipulate the password directly.

1. Find your database:

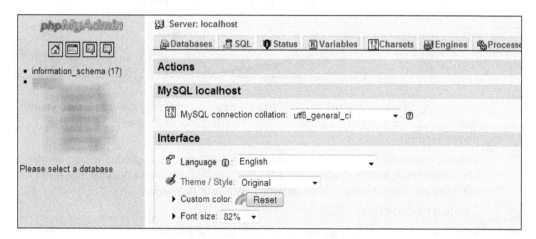

2. The databases will be on the left side of this screen. Choose yours.
3. Once you do, you'll see the database tables listed as follows:

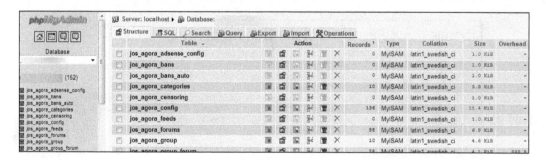

4. Locate `jos_users`.

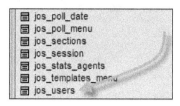

5. Scroll down on the left until you see `jos_users`. This will likely be near the bottom.

6. Locate your super user; it will be user type Super Administrator.

id	name	username	email	password	usertype
67	Bill Smith	B8388A	Bill.smith@domain.com	587393209xxw939a30vvc3f003asf32azL:UalvEXnnKr4.	Super Administrator

Depending on how many users are setup on your site, you may need to locate yours by scrolling. In any event locate the Super Administrator field. It will look like the above example.

You see the ARROW? That's the password that has been encrypted. The combination of numbers and letters is known as a "HASH". Joomla! is able to decode that and compare the stored copy of the password, with your password.

7. Create a new password HASH.

To do this, you'll need to visit this very handy tool located at:

`http://www.tooljo.com/joomla-15-password-hash-generator`

The tool can take your password and convert it to the proper "hash" that Joomla! will use.

8. Enter your password in the first box and then click **Execute command**. This generates the new 'hash' at the bottom.

9. Edit the user in the MySQL database.

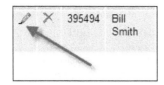

10. Clicking the pencil icon, on the user you wish to edit will open it up.

    Now you'll see something like this partial screenshot.

| | | Browse | Structure | SQL | Search | Insert | Export | Import | Operations | Empty |

Field	Type	Function		Null	Value
id	int(11)		▼		395494
name	varchar(255)		▼		Bill Smith
username	varchar(150)		▼		B8388A
email	varchar(100)		▼		bill.smith@domain.com
password	varchar(100)		▼		137ab7dd6c4300c56be9431b96bdf501:mNO

The **Value** column on the right and the **password** row is the one we want to change.

- Remove all the data in the password value field by deleting it. Next return to the MD5 Creation Webpage where you created your password/hash and copy that HASH (highlight and *Ctrl+C* for Windows users).

- Return here and paste it into the password value field. (*Ctrl+V* for Windows users).

- Click **Go** in the lower-right corner.

- Go back into `jos_users` and you'll see the password hash has changed:

Field	Type	Function		Null	Value
id	int(11)		▼		395494
name	varchar(255)		▼		Bill Smith
username	varchar(150)		▼		B8388A
email	varchar(100)		▼		bill.smith@domain.com
password	varchar(100)		▼		79a950b3482a218f82bc2d5552461289:Fgaq

- You can at this time, if necessary, change the email address as well. Be sure and click **Go** every time.

- Once complete, close your browser. This will log you out of phpMyadmin.

How it works...

Joomla! is by its nature a database-driven website. In other words, everything it does in terms of users, content, and many other actions are tied into the database.

By storing the content and passwords, it allows users to change content without programming. One word of caution, unless you are an expert, do not change anything else in the database. Doing so could render your site useless or damaged.

As you can see - attempting to decipher it from the database is next to impossible. The password hash is nearly impossible (not impossible but almost) to break. It uses the MD5 function of PHP to encrypt the password, and it adds 'SALT' to it, which is extra data meant to increase the complexity of the password.

What we did in this example is we literally went around the normal Joomla! procedure for changing a password.

Sometime you might do this would be if a developer has locked you out. Or something has corrupted a portion of your database, rendering the Admin password unreadable.

Once you make this change in the database, it's immediate. You can then return to the `domain.com/administrator` link and login.

Again, changing ANY password in Joomla! can be done using this method.

Pass the salt please

Passwords in Joomla! are encrypted using a mathematical formula called "MD5" but with the added benefit of some 'random' data added at the time you create a password. This random data is called SALT.

6
Managing Modules and Components

In this chapter, we will cover:

- ▶ Installing and managing components
- ▶ Installing, creating and managing modules
- ▶ Creating menu items for components
- ▶ Enabling, disabling, and uninstalling extensions
- ▶ Changing the menu order of a component

Introduction

Joomla! is known as a 'framework' and it is extendable, or in other words, can be added to, with small programs known as 'extensions'. A specific class of those is known as modules and components.

Modules are small applets. They present information on the site to the user. They can be used in a variety of positions and are typically very simple to use and configure.

Components are full-fledged applications and are much more complex. They can only (usually) be displayed within the main area of the page. The typical component requires a menu item to link to it.

Each adds to Joomla! in some fashion that adds functionality or allows better interaction with users.

Modules are not to be confused with module positions in a template. They do work hand–in–hand, but are not the same. When you think of module positions, think that this is where they fit. Modules are assigned and fit into module positions.

In this chapter, we'll explore the installation, assignment, and in the case of modules, the creation of modules. Along the way, we'll learn about some finer points of each.

Installing and managing components

Starting with Joomla! 1.5.0, the installer became "Universal" - or more easily said, you go to the same place to install your extensions, templates, plugins, and so forth. Each of the add-on programs are managed from different menus, but installed from the same place.

There is, like most things in Joomla!, more than one way to do something. Installation is no different.

Each 'extension' usually starts with a special prefix that helps you identify what it is. Here are two examples from some third-party developers.

▶ `com_securelive.zip`: Installs SECUREJOOMLA which is a third-party security component for Joomla!

▶ `mod_corephp_weather`: Installs the quick and elegant local weather information for your users with the 'corePHP' Weather Module.

Getting ready

As we're going to be going through a couple of examples, I have downloaded a couple of different programs. You'll need to have on hand a component to install. We'll be installing Agora Forum. You can download a copy of it at no charge from `http://www.jvitals.com`.

How to do it...

Installing a component.

1. Login to your Administrator Console.
2. Click **Extensions | Install/Uninstall**.

Once you are in here you'll have a few options to choose from:

There are three methods to install, in this section we'll focus on the first method. We'll examine the other two in a moment.

3. Click **Browse...** and find the file. Typically, your browser will have a default location such as **Download** in the **Documents** directory. This will vary by operating system and browser.

4. Click **Upload File & Install**.

In this case, I have uploaded com_agora_3.0.13.zip, which contains the full Agora Forum. Upon a successful **Upload File & Install** you'll see this.

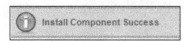

This indicates it has been installed.

But what about this?

This indicates you have already installed the extension. You'll need to remove it or delete from the database. See Troubleshooting for more information.

From here you can manage your component and interact with it. To do so, from the Administrator Console, click **Components**, and find the component in question.

How it works...

The installation manager opens up the `ZIP` file and reviews the content and installs it onto your site. It will create the appropriate entries in the database.

Some extensions that are not coded with the auto-installer will not work with this process. Those should not be in the main stream, but be aware.

Additionally it allows you to interact with the extension by creating a menu item.

Now that we have installed the **Agora Forum**, we'll want to manage it. In this case, the Agora is a component (remember `com_agora_3.0.13.zip` in our install?)

In the administrator click **Components | Agora Forum**.

In case of Agora forum there are many submenus from which I can configure, control, and maintain this component. Each component will have different menus.

Here's another example:

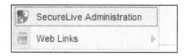

In this example when I pulled down to the **SecureLive Administration** Console, there are no submenus off of the main menu. The menus are actually in the application once you open it.

There's more...

Now let's talk about some other options, or possibly some pieces of general information that are relevant to this task.

Uninstalling a component

A good thumb-rule for security is to completely remove components and other extensions you do not need. That way in the event that vulnerability is discovered, you won't be exposed. Another potential issues is conflicts between other extensions. While rare, it can happen. So generally, if you aren't using a component, remove it.

1. Login to your Administrator Console.

2. Click **Extensions | Install/Uninstall**.

3. Click **Components**.

   You'll need to locate your extension you wish to remove from the list. In this case, our example is highlighted in the following screenshot:

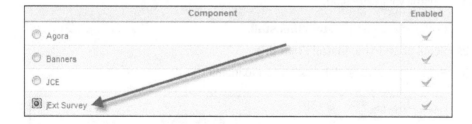

4. Select the extension you wish to uninstall by clicking the radio button.

5. Next in the upper right-hand side, click **Uninstall**.

You should see this message upon a successful uninstall.

Disabling a component

Occasionally a component does not need to be removed, but merely turned off. This process is known as "disabling".

1. Click **Extensions | Install/Uninstall** (This is the **Extension Manager**)
2. Click **Components**.

   You'll see in the case of Agora and others - something like this:

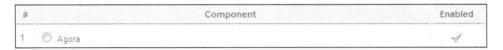

   As you can see there is a green check showing it is **Enabled**.

3. Click the green check to disable it.

   Now the Agora extension is disabled and cannot be used. You can click the red circle **x** to enable it again.

Installing from a URL

Sometimes a developer will keep their latest code available from a download. This is a simple means to install your extension.

1. Click **Extensions | Install/Uninstall**.
2. Scroll down to the **Install From URL**.
3. Put in the address of the extension to install.

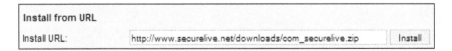

4. Click **Install** and if it was successful you'll get this:

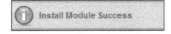

Creating menu items for components

In a previous recipe, you learned how to install a component. That's exactly half the process. Next you create a menu item for it. This will enable it to interact with the users.

Carrying on with our Agora example, let's create a menu for Agora so our WidgetWorld Users can post threads on the products.

How to do it...

1. Log in to your Administrator Console.
2. Click **Menus** and choose the menu you wish - in this case, use **Main Menu** - thus **Menus | Main Menu**.
3. Click **New** in the upper right-hand corner.

The above screenshot is a snippet of the **Select Menu Item Type** - Yours will vary. In this example, we see several items - we want **Agora Forum**.

4. Click **Agora Forum**.
5. Scroll down and fill out the details as you see here (use your own details):

This will give the forum menu on the home page a title called **WidgetWorld FORUM**.

6. Click **Save**.

Now when we visit this from the front of the site we see the completed **WidgetWorld FORUM** on our menu:

How it works...

The creation and location for the component is stored in the database. When the Joomla! template renders the page, it will include the component.

Thus - when you create a menu item for the component you are giving the user the ability to 'use' the component.

There's more...

As you gain more experience with Joomla!, you'll want to work with the menu to give it a more custom feel. Let's look at changing the location of menus.

Changing the location of the menu

You likely noted that the forum in the last example was at the bottom of the **Main Menu**. Let's change the order.

1. Click **Menu | Main Menu** - see the **Order** column.

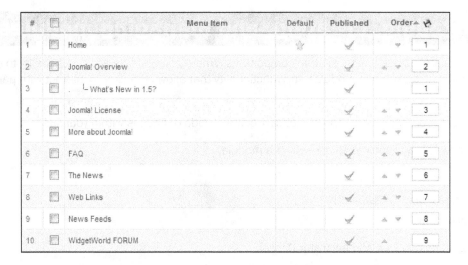

#		Menu Item	Default	Published	Order▲ 🖫
1		Home	☆	✓	▽	1
2		Joomla! Overview		✓	▲ ▽	2
3		└ What's New in 1.5?		✓		1
4		Joomla! License		✓	▲ ▽	3
5		More about Joomla!		✓	▲ ▽	4
6		FAQ		✓	▲ ▽	5
7		The News		✓	▲ ▽	6
8		Web Links		✓	▲ ▽	7
9		News Feeds		✓	▲ ▽	8
10		WidgetWorld FORUM		✓	▲	9

This is the order of display.

2. Type **2** in the **Order** number box for the **WidgetWorld FORUM**.

3. Click the Floppy disk <save> icon next to **Order** - the result should be as you see in the following screenshot:

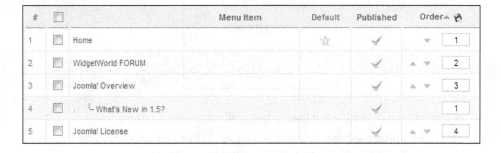

#		Menu Item	Default	Published	Order▲ 🖫
1		Home	☆	✓	▽	1
2		WidgetWorld FORUM		✓	▲ ▽	2
3		Joomla! Overview		✓	▲ ▽	3
4		└ What's New in 1.5?		✓		1
5		Joomla! License		✓	▲ ▽	4

Here are the menus before and after side-by-side:

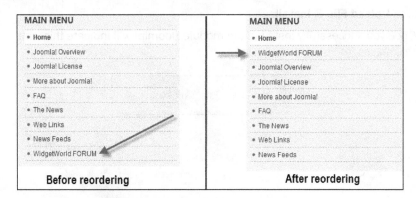

Before reordering   After reordering

Installing, creating, and managing modules

Modules are a larger 'catch all' than components. Where components add functionality to the Joomla! core framework, modules add functionality that allows the user to interact with parts of the system.

Other types of modules are those that can 'contain' code or images within your site.

In this recipe, we'll look at all aspects of a module.

How to do it...

Installing a Module

1. Login to your Administrator Console.

2. Click **Extensions | Install/Uninstall**.

    Once you are in here, you'll have a few options to choose from:

    There are three methods to install a module, in this section we'll focus on the first method. We'll examine the other two in a moment.

3. Click **Browse...** and find the file.

4. Click **Upload File & Install**.

    Once you successfully installed the module, Joomla! will indicate this with this message:

How it works...

Module installation is a very similar process to components. The Joomla! universal installer has made it very simple.

The installer will write the appropriate settings to the database and will copy the files down to their respective locations.

There's more...

There comes a time when you no longer need a module. Or you may wish to disable it or even create a new one that didn't exist before.

As modules are essentially very lightweight in nature, creating them and placing them is easy.

The next few recipes cover these items.

Deleting modules

There are two methods to delete a module.

METHOD 1:

1. Click **Extensions | Install/Uninstall**.
2. Click **Modules**.
3. Check the module you wish to delete.

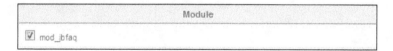

4. Once you check the module(s) you wish to delete, click **Uninstall** in the upper right-hand side:

Once you successfully uninstall the module, Joomla! will indicate this with this message:

METHOD 2:

1. Click **Extensions | Module Manager**.

2. Check the module you wish to delete.

3. Click **Delete** in the upper right-hand side, the key difference is the message:

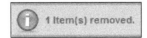

Disabling modules

Like components, occasionally, you need to disable a module. There are two methods to do this.

DISABLING A SINGLE MODULE:

1. Click **Extensions | Module Manager**.

2. Click the green arrow of the module.

DISABLING MULTIPLE MODULES:

1. Click **Extensions | Module Manager**.

2. Click the checkbox to the left of the name of the modules you wish to disable.

3. In the upper right-hand side, click **Disable**.

You may also enable a single or multiple modules using this method.

Create new modules

In this recipe, we'll look at the **New** module function. This is not the same as 'coding' a module.

There are several different types of 'new' modules you can add. These can be enabled, disabled, and treated like any other modules. The process to create them is the same, so we'll focus in on a special module type called **Custom HTML**.

This module can do quite a bit.

1. Click **Extensions | Install/Uninstall**.

2. Click **Module Manager**.

3. Click **New** - this will take you to the **Module | New function**.

4. Choose the **Custom HTML** radio button.

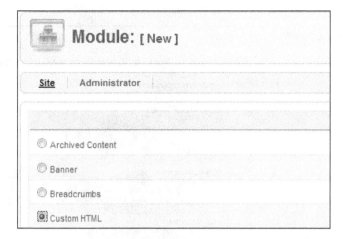

5. Click **Next** in the upper right-hand side.
6. This will take you into a detailed screen with plenty of options. Let's review each as we build it.

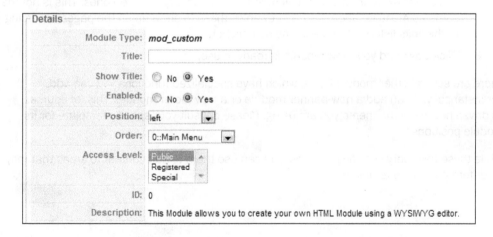

- ❑   **Title**: Name the module as you wish (this is publicly viewable)
- ❑   **Show Title**: **No** or **Yes**
- ❑   **Enabled**: **No** or **Yes** (to use it must be enabled)
- ❑   **Position**: This is where in the template you want it to be seen
- ❑   **Order**: What 'order' does it need to appear in on the menus. The module positions dictate what order they appear if there is more than one. For instance, if you have three in module position left, then this will arrange them according to the order.

❑ **Access Level**: Choose the level of access needed to use/interact with module

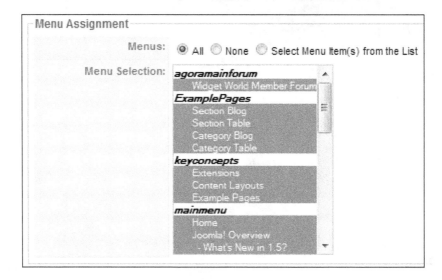

7. You can show your module on all menu items, none, or selected ones. This is not the same as menu creation. Rather it enables these to show up on the pages according to the links listed in the preceding screenshot.

8. Click **Save** and your new module is ready to use.

There are several other module types, which have specialized functions you can add. For instance, you can add a new banner module or a new footer module. This, of course, is driven heavily by the theme you are using. Please consult your specific template for its module positions.

While these have very specific functions, you can use them to add content to areas that may be different than the template.

7
Managing Articles Using the K2 Content Construction Kit

In this chapter, we will cover:

- ▸ Installation of K2 content creation kit
- ▸ Configuration of K2
- ▸ Setting up a master category in K2 to ease your administration time
- ▸ Extras for K2 such as YouTube feeds and photo galleries
- ▸ Importing your Joomla! content into K2
- ▸ Setup and configuration of categories and sub-categories
- ▸ Using the K2 Tag Cloud
- ▸ Configuration and moderation of commenting system
- ▸ Overall tips and tricks to make your K2 site work

Introduction

Generally speaking, a basic article is a simple matter to create and manage. When a site gets large with a lot of articles, it can be unwieldy. This need is filled by a **Content Construction Kit** or **CCK**. Several good CCK's exist in the Joomlasphere and each has its own unique means to accomplish the task of content management and creation.

For our purposes we'll look at the CCK known as K2.

K2 provides you an integrated solution that features rich content forms - extending the basic article. This is an article with additional fields that can contain the article images, videos, image galleries or even attachments. Add nested-level categories and tags to that, and you have a very powerful system.

In this chapter we'll look at the installation and use of K2.

Installation and introduction of K2

In this recipe you will go through the steps to install and configure K2 in your Joomla! site.

Getting ready

You will want to download K2 from the following URL: `http://getk2.org`

Additionally, you may want to have a development site to install and learn this on rather than your production site.

How to do it...

1. Installation of K2 works like any other Joomla! extension.
2. Be sure and backup your files and database before beginning - this way you can easily roll back should something go wrong.
3. Download K2.
4. Log in to your Joomla! site as the Super Administrator.
5. Click **Extensions | Install / Uninstall**.
6. Browse, locate, and upload the K2 package.
7. Install.

   Installation of K2 should be complete.

 If you are not running the Joom!Fish language translation extension on your site, you will see an informational message stating that K2 did not install the content elements. Joom!Fish is used to translate your site into other languages. If you have no plans on using this, then ignore the message.

Now when you go to **Components**, you'll see the K2 icon. Clicking it will show you this screen:

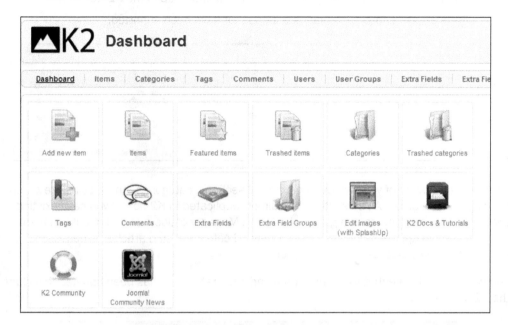

8. The next step is to bring all of our current content (articles, media, and so on) into K2.

9. While in the K2 Dashboard, look at the upper right-hand side for the **Import Joomla! content** button.

You will see this message (or a similar one depending on your K2 version):

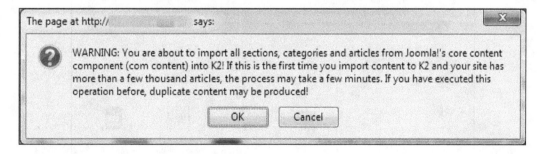

10. Click **Ok** to start the process.

11. Once complete, you'll see all your content now shows up in the **K2 Items** menu. Here are the sample Joomla! data items that have been imported.

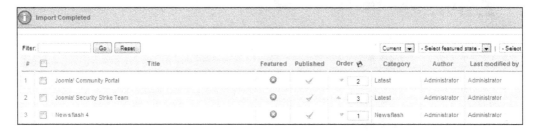

Keep in mind that all of your pre-existing Joomla! sections, categories, and articles are still in the core Joomla! areas. All these items are simply duplicated in K2 now. If you have existing content take a few minutes and go into the Article Manager of Joomla! and unpublish them. You may need to update menu links to your new K2 categories and articles as necessary which will be discussed later in this chapter.

Additionally, you'll note that the main Joomla! administrator page has been updated to include the K2 dashboard.

Further configuration of K2.

K2 has a powerful, nested-category system. It offers you the ability to configure in detail, each category, allowing any category to inherit from another category's parameter settings.

Let's use this feature of K2 to configure a master category that will allow other categories to inherit the settings. This means you can change one category and affect them all at the same time – which is quite time-saving.

A word of caution, this could impact your search engine-friendly URLs depending on the extension you use to create them.

1. Open the K2 Dashboard.
2. Select **Categories**.
3. Click **New** in the upper right-hand side.
4. Fill in the following details:

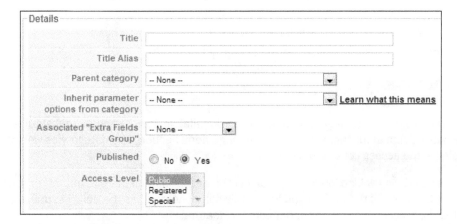

- ❑ **Title** is the title of your category
- ❑ **Title Alias** is the internal reference
- ❑ **Parent category** should be left as **–None–** - all other categories will inherit from this category
- ❑ **Inherit parameter options from category** should be left as **–None–**
- ❑ **Associated "Extra Fields" Group** should be left as **None**.
- ❑ **Published** is **Yes**
- ❑ **Access Level** is **Public**

I have filled mine out and the following screenshot is the completed **Details** section. For now, this is all you'll need to do. Later recipes will utilize this:

This is my master category that all other categories will seek out their parameters from. The reason for this will be clear shortly.

When you have finished, save the category.

How it works...

K2 is nearly a content management system, like Joomla!, in itself. It actually substitutes many of the native Joomla! functions like article management, section, and category as well as providing some access control functions.

When using K2, you will no longer use many of the native Joomla! menus, but rather you will use the K2 version of the tools. If you install this component, it has the ability to pull in all the data (users, articles) into K2 through the import feature.

There's more...

In the previous recipe, we set up a master category; now we'll configure it here.

Configuration of your master category

The following screenshot shows a new category created, which is the child of the master category. Thus, it will inherit its settings from the master.

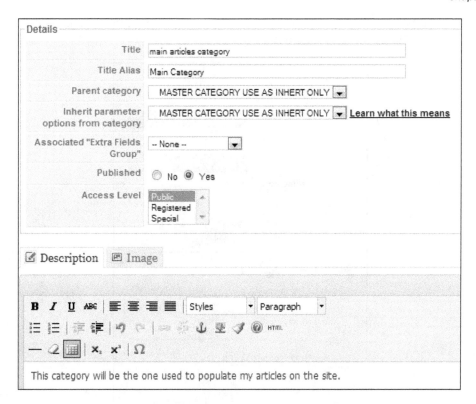

Never assign anything to the master category, always set up a new category for articles, sections, blogs, or other content. You can then tweak the individual categories based on their own requirements.

The two important parts of the details in this category are the **Parent category** and **Inherit parameter options from category**. These can be set for different options and using the master category is a style choice, not a technical one.

What this tells our new category is that it should inherit its parameters from the master.

Revisiting our master category, we can see there are many, many options to choose from. Continuing on let's set up our parameters.

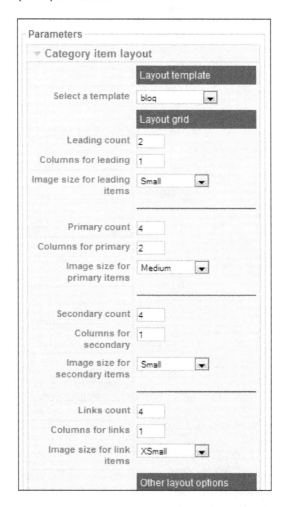

The extreme right shows all our parameter settings in the category. Due to the number of different parameters, this will be broken down into several images.

Under the layout template, I have selected and installed a third-party K2 template from the site `http://www.k2joom.com`. In our example, I am building a 'blog' style website, and will use separate categories to represent different potential authors on the site. All will use the Blog template from `K2Joom.com` and as such, I have the 'blog' selected in the template field. The rest of the fields deal with columns and leading articles, and so on. The defaults are fine.

The rest of that column shows this:

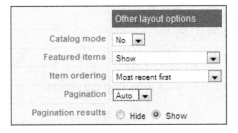

Next up is **Category view options**.

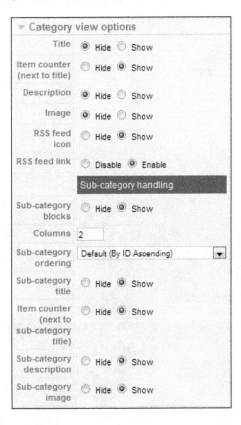

Most of these are self-explanatory, however I want to point out to you that the **Title** should be disabled, or, it will show the category title, in the website.

Each category that inherits its parameters from the master category can be set individually. However, consider if the changes would be better made in the master category, thus changing all inherited categories. For example, you have the ability to define multiple master categories to fine tune your inherited categories.

Master category one has the following inherited categories:

- ▸ Sub-category - Blog on Surfboards
- ▸ Sub-category - Blog on water skis

Each of these has specific settings that match their content.

Master category two has the following inherited categories:

- ▸ Sub-category - Blog on politics
- ▸ Sub-category - Blog on current world events

In these cases, you could tweak just the master categories and touch all the subcategories. The simple advantage for you is it is time-saving.

Item image options.

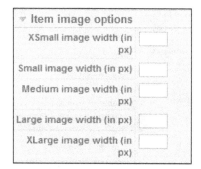

The next set of parameters allows for images to be set by px size. This will vary strictly by your site and content.

Item view options in category listings.

There are many options in this section; so again we'll break it down into a couple of images to make it easier to follow:

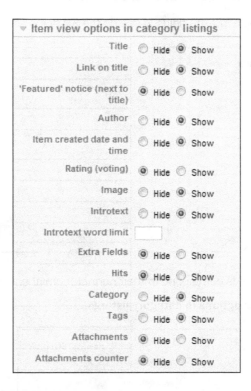

Some of these will be familiar and others will be new to you. The primary choices I want to point out to you are:

▸ **'Featured' notice (next to title)**: If this is turned on, it displays a nice corner banner on the right upper-corner of the article. This grabs the readers' attention.

▸ **Extra Fields - Hide** or **Show**: This will hide or show any 'extra fields' that have been added. If you use only one master category, I suggest you refrain from putting extra fields in the master category. Rather, put it in the inherited category. This setting will show them or hide them.

Here is an example of extra fields in use on the K2 demo site.

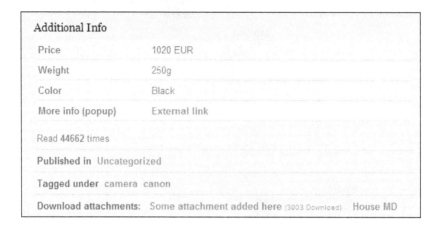

The rest of the fields correspond to their normal Joomla! equivalents.

Second half of Item view options in category listings.

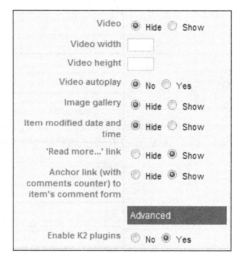

▸ **Video**: The Video **Hide** or **Show** corresponds to any video content you put into K2.

▸ **Enable K2 plugins**: It corresponds to the earlier reference of all videos and simple image gallery. This should be set to **Yes**.

The rest of the items are self-explanatory and can be left as default unless you have other requirements. Then you may change them to fit your needs.

The last option field has many choices and will be displayed in multiple images.

Item view options.

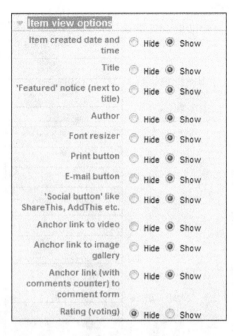

Again, most of these are self-explanatory and I'll hit the highlights.

- ▶ **Social button:** This adds a very nice set of buttons for your visitors to employ social media through your site. This includes Twitter, Facebook, Delicious, Digg, Reddit, StumbleUpon, MySpace, and Technorati.

- ▶ **Rating (voting):** This is to allow people to vote on the article or content.

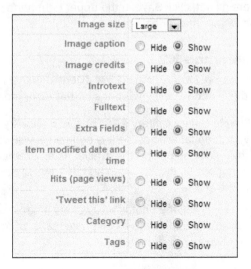

- ▸ **'Tweet this' link**: This will take the visitors over to their Twitter accounts to share your site with their followers.

- ▸ **Extra Fields**: Shows or hides the extra fields on the article. Extra fields give you the ability to add in any extra information you need. Such as price, weight, color, length, width, and so on.

This is the final part of the long list of configurable items. Most, if not all, should be self-explanatory.

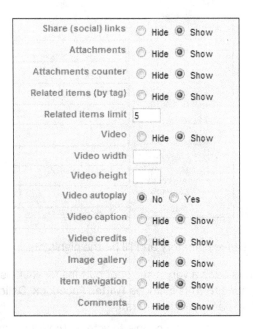

Now that these are all set, click **Save** in the upper right-hand side. This completes the configuration of your master category.

Extra options to enhance K2

The developers of K2, JoomlaWorks.gr offer a few extensions that are top in the categories they exist in. Integrating these into K2 will give your site that extra professional touch.

- ▸ **JoomlaWorks "Simple Image Gallery PRO" plugin**: It allows you to add image galleries inside your Joomla! articles. As it is a plugin, it will work within articles by simply giving a quick code snippet in the article. As an example, if I had a number of images of automobiles on display, I can add this {gallery}autophotos{/gallery} inside the article.

This extension will display all the photos as a gallery. In this example, everything uploaded from autophotos displays as an image gallery. You can obtain this plugin from JoomlaWorks.gr

- **AllVideos** plugin: This allows you to embed online-streaming videos inside your articles. Your video and audio content can reside on your own server or an outside server.

  One common usage model is to upload a video, say about your company, to YouTube and then use this to display that video on your site.

  Here is an actual example showing how a YouTube video, is being 'displayed' on the site `SalvusAlerting.com`. The bandwidth is consumed over at YouTube, but shown on their site.

When these two plugins are installed on your Joomla! site, K2 will automatically detect it and will allow the use of these in K2. It is a low cost, but high-reward setup.

Extra fields and groups

K2 has an interesting feature called extra fields and extra groups. Think of these as mini-custom forms you can add to the content. A typical use would be in the catalogue mode of K2. It does work well for things like, author biography on magazine articles or product catalogue extra information such as weight, size, color.

In each article, you can select the group and fields to add. This offers many combinations limited by your imagination. The use of extra fields is completely optional.

Adding extra field groups:

1. Open up K2 Dashboard.
2. Click **Extra Fields** group.
3. Click **New**.
4. Add your group name (example: **Products Group**).
5. Save.

    You've created a group to hold your extra fields. Next you will want to create the extra fields.

Adding extra fields:

1. Open up K2 Dashboard.
2. Click **Extra Fields**.
3. Click **New**.
4. Add the name of the **Extra Fields** in **Name** (example: **Widget Specs**).
5. Click **Published Yes**.
6. Pull down the **Group** (example: Products Group) and choose the correct group or you can create a new group here.
7. Next choose the type of field you want:

    ❏ **Text Field**: Displays a single field for text

    ❏ **Text Area**: It is a large field for text that spans several lines

    ❏ **Drop-down Selection list**: Provides you any number of fields, allowing you to prepopulate. When you create your article, you can select from the list. Again an example is size, weight, color, and so on.

    ❏ **Multi-select list**: Allows you to do a multiple selection from a list.

    ❏ **Radio buttons**: This is the traditional select 'one' from a list of many.

    ❏ **Link text**: Allows you to offer a URL with display text, and controls to open a new window or stay in the same window.

    ❏ **CSV Data**: Upload of CSV data - great for pricing - you can have a single file loaded with pricing. Change the one file in your extra fields, and the pricing would change automatically across your site.

Using the extra fields and groups.

Recall that we said a master category can be the overall place holder for your site's settings. It allows you to update settings globally in your site, without touching every article. It allows you to update settings in inherited categories in your site, without touching every article.

You may not want to set your extra fields and extra groups at the master category level but rather choose a subcategory that covers that information.

Taking our concept of a product website we may have something as follows:

Title	Order▲ ✍		Associated extra field groups
MASTER CATEGORY USE AS INHERT ONLY (1)	▲ ▼	6	
└ main New articles (0)	▼	1	
└ Product Pricing and Specifications (0)	▲	2	Product Pricing

This screenshot shows the master category used to globally specify our parameters. The other two categories **main New articles** and **Product Pricing and Specifications** are subcategories. Notice the **Associated extra fields groups**. That tells K2 to allow the use of the **Product Pricing** extra fields in all articles created in that category. Anytime you create an article, assign it to this group, and include those fields, they will be displayed. Using our **CSV field**, you can update pricing once - in the extra fields section and it will update all your articles.

One tip to recall, if you have not assigned extra fields to a category, articles created in that category will not display the fields.

Working with items AKA articles

The power of K2 is in the idea of categorizing your data, thus making it easier to manage. This will be especially helpful as your site grows in content. Many sites are fully article-based and it is not uncommon to see a site with thousands of articles on it.

In this section, we'll tackle some more category-specific recipes.

You may have noticed by now that data does not show up as typical articles do in Joomla!. In other words, if you added an item, set it published and featured, it may not be displayed on your site because you have not set up a menu item to your K2 content.

K2 will need to be added to your menu structure to display the items (articles) in K2.

The first recipe will take into account a site that has been in operation for a while and has K2 added to it.

Getting ready

This section assumes you have installed K2 and have content on your site.

How to do it...

1. Make sure you have a full backup of the database and the files.
2. Log in as the administrator.
3. Open the K2 Dashboard.
4. If you DID NOT import your content in, (see the first recipe), do so now.

> If you have ALREADY imported your content using the **Import Joomla! Content** button - DO NOT import again. You run the risk of duplicating all your content. Should this happen, you can go in and delete the duplicate items. This can be a time-consuming process.

5. Open **Article Manager | Content | Article Manager**.
6. Select all your articles from the **Article Manager** and unpublish.
7. Open **Menu Manager** and find your **Home** menu.

    Now that we have unpublished content, we'll need to replace the traditional Joomla! content items with K2 content. Opening the **Menu Manager** and selecting the **Home** menu item will show this:

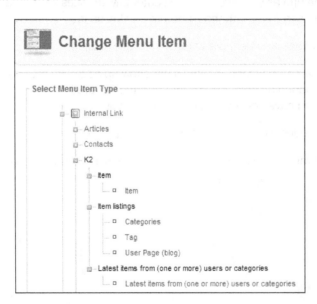

As you can see under K2 there are several choices to display content on your site. I will choose **Item | Item** as my display mode. This will show my visitors content in article form.

You can pick what works best for you. Now returning to the instructions:

8. After choosing **Menu Item Type** - click **Save**.

9. Open K2 Dashboard.

10. Select **Items**.

Here is a partial screenshot of the items in our sample site.

Title	Featured	Published	Order ⬏	Category
Mikes Article	⊗	✓	1	MASTER CATEGORY USE AS INHERT ONLY
Chapter form	✓	✓	1	chapter form
This is a new K2 article	✓	✓	1	New K2 Category for Joomla! cookbook
Joomla! Community Portal	⊗	⊗	▽ 2	Latest
Joomla! Security Strike Team	⊗	⊗	▲ 3	Latest
Newsflash 4	⊗	⊗	▽ 1	Newsflash

As you can see, it now starts to take on a bit more traditional Joomla! look. I can choose featured articles, publish them, or note. Set the order they show up in, the category they belong to and more.

When you import content, from Joomla!, the articles retain their identity from **Section and Category** configuration. For example, the **Joomla! Community Portal** listed in the preceding screenshot as belonging to the category **Latest** has a parent category of **News**.

When you imported the content, sections became the new K2 top-level categories. All existing categories become subcategories of the new top level categories. As we added K2 to a working site with sections and category data already in place, I want to make sure they inherit from our master category.

In our sample site, we see the following screen when we open the K2 categories from the K2 Dashboard:

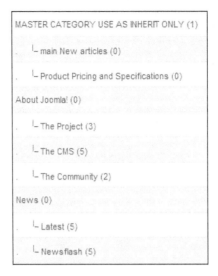

We instruct the new top-level categories to follow the master category as the model for the rest. The following instructions will show you how.

1. Open K2 Dashboard.

2. Click **Categories**.

3. Open your imported top-level categories - for this site it's **About Joomla!** and **News**. Each of these has sub-categories.

4. Click **About Joomla!** (or your equivalent).

5. Change the **Inherit parameter options from category** to **MASTER CATEGORY USE AS INHERIT ONLY**.

6. Make sure the **Parent category** stays set to **–None--**.

7. Click **Save**.

When done, it will look like this:

> **Extra fields**
>
> Did you notice the **Associated "Extra Fields Group"** is set to **- None -** ? You can change this parent category group to use an extra fields group and still keep the master category parameters.

Each of the subcategories will inherit from the master category.

By doing this, you can still control all the categories parameters simply by changing the master category.

How it works...

The category system as described here for K2 is a giant access-control system allowing you the flexibility to structure your site and data as you need. It also offers a means to control the 'look and feel' of the articles from a central place.

When you import a Joomla! site into K2 you bring all the sections, content, articles, and other associated parts into it.

Sections become new parent categories and the old categories become subcategories. This can be a bit confusing at first. One suggestion is to write out on paper what you want the site to look like, and then lay out your categories. You might find that the structure you had can be more user-friendly using K2 and you will want to change.

This category system offers you nearly unlimited means to nest articles. In essence, a category can have unlimited categories under it. There is a limit to this in terms of management, but you get the idea.

There's more...

Using tags in K2 will give you the ability to improve your **Search Engine Optimization** or **SEO** on your site. Additionally, the use of tags will allow you to give your users the ability to follow the tags to other articles. In this section we'll review how to use Tags in K2.

Tags are keywords or terms that are assigned to your content. This enables your visitors to quickly locate what they need by one word descriptions.

Using Tags in K2

Tags can be created before an article is written or on the fly. I prefer on the fly as it will match the article. You can think of a tag almost as a dynamic index. Every time a tag is added to an article, it will show up in the **K2 Tag Cloud** module if you are using it. The more a single tag, such as Joomla!, is used in the content, the larger it appears in the K2 Cloud module.

K2 Tag Clouds can benefit your search engine optimization and a navigational element.

Here is an example of our **K2 Tag Cloud**:

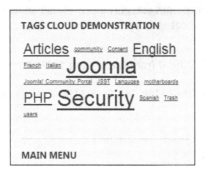

This is an image of our **K2 Tag Cloud** module. The more often a tag is added to an article, the larger it appears.

Setting up your site for Tag Clouds:

K2 installs the **K2 Tools** module by default. The module has many functions, but for our purposes here, we'll use the **Tag** module.

1. Log in to the Administrator Console of Joomla!.
2. Click **Extensions | Module Manager**.
3. Click **New** to create a new module.
4. Find this for your new item:

5. Once in there, give it a name and select its module location.
6. On the right under **Parameters**, pull down the **Select module functionality** drop-down list as follows:

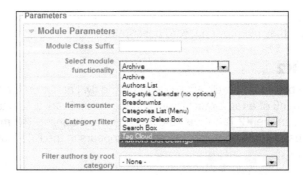

7. Select **Tag Cloud** as shown in the preceding screenshot.

8. Leave all the root categories set for none - this will enable K2 to pull in all the categories.

9. Click **Save**.

 This particular module, has many functions and you can set up a new module to use any of the great tools built into it.

Next you will want to add some tags to articles. As I said at the beginning of this article, you have two different ways to do this. You may add them to the article or you may add them to the **Tag Manager**. Let's quickly review the latter method.

1. Open K2 Dashboard.

2. Click **Tags**.

3. You may see a list of tags there. If you wish to delete them, simply check the ones you want to remove and click **Delete** in the upper right-hand corner. Otherwise just leave them.

4. Click **New** which will open the **Details** box. Fill in the tag; make sure it's published and click **Save**. This is an example of a filled out tag box (before save).

Adding Tags on the fly:

This model allows you to tag the content as soon as you create it. If there are tags available, already such as those from the previous step, then you can add them.

1. Open K2 Dashboard.

2. Click **Items**.

3. Select an item or click **New** to create an item.

4. The field **Tags** will be blank, you can start to type in a field, such as **K2 Content Creation Kit** (as shown in the preceding screenshot). If it exists, then it will be available to be able to click and add.

5. If there are no tags available, then simply type one in and click **Return** or add a comma.

6. Here is an example item with tags.

Here we have four tags, **Security x, PHP x, Joomla x, K2 Content Creation Kit x**. Any item (article) that has these tags will be easily found by both users and search bots.

Let's see how our Tag Cloud looks now:

You probably notice the changes, especially the addition of the new tag **K2 Content Creation Kit**. Clicking on that tag will yield two articles, and clicking on the **Security** tag yields three. Search engines can follow these links to better categorize your site. Users can get a sense of what is more important in terms of content from your site and it helps them navigate.

Closing on this, I strongly suggest you spend time picking tags that are important on your site and is relevant to the purpose of it.

Working with comments

Your site may be one such as a blog that allows visitors to comment on the articles. It may be a product site, which seeks customer feedback. Or you may just want people to leave a comment.

K2 has you covered in all these scenarios and more. The built-in comment system is easy to use and requires little configuration.

How to do it...

Enabling comments in a category.

You first need to decide if commenting will be allowed GLOBALLY or by certain categories or items. Let's examine all three methods.

Globally:

If you used the master category method then you can make this change quickly and easily.

1. Open K2 Dashboard.
2. Open **Categories**.
3. Open your master category category.
4. Scroll down on your right (**Parameters**) and select **Item view options**.
5. Scroll down to the option shown as follows:

6. To allow **Comments** to be given globally check **Show**.
7. To disallow **Comments** to be given globally check **Hide**.

   Each of these can be overridden at the sub-category and Item level.

Top level and sub-categories.

1. Open K2 Dashboard.
2. Open **Categories**.
3. Open your chosen top level category or sub-category.
4. Scroll down on your right (**Parameters**) and select **Item view options**.
5. Click **Hide** or **Show** to display it on items in this top Level or sub-category

Enabling comments by Item.

There might be specific Items (articles) you wish to turn commenting on for, but leave it off for the entirety of the site. Follow these steps to enable it by ITEM:

1. Open the K2 Dashboard.

2. Click **Items**.

3. Find the item you wish to enable commenting for.

4. In the **Parameters** on the right, open **Item view options**.

5. Scroll down till you see this:

6. To allow **Comments** to be left on this item, select **Show**.

How it works...

K2 has a great commenting system that is fully integrated with the rest of the CCK. This gives you all the tools you need to enable commenting in articles, products, news articles, products, or wherever your imagination takes you.

The K2 system is built to be very granular and allows global, top-level, or sub-category and item-level support. The great thing about this is, the commenting can be over ridden at any level.

Moving to the next section, it's one thing to let people leave a comment but managing them is the next task.

Configuring comments

Invariably if you allow comments on a public site, you'll get the occasional ad for 'watches' or 'prescription med'. You're likely to get someone leaving inappropriate comments. Using a human verification tool such as a Captcha extension can mitigate most of this.

Moderating comments.

First, you will want to set up your particular parameters within the commenting system. K2 allows comments to be published automatically by default. I would recommend you to disable that.

1. Open K2 Dashboard.

2. Select **Comments**.

3. Select **Parameters** in upper right-hand side.

4. Scroll down in **Parameters** to the section called **Comments**. It will look like this:

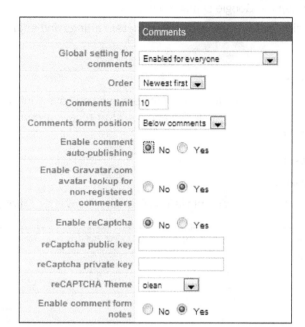

There are many settings in parameters, but for our purpose let's focus on these few for now.

▶ **Global setting for comments**: Your choices are:

- ❑ **Disabled**
- ❑ **Enabled for everyone**
- ❑ **Enabled for Registered Users Only**

▶ **Enable comment auto-publishing**: Again, this is the default, but if you leave it on, any posted comment will show up immediately. That could be dangerous.

▶ **Enable Gravatar.com avatar lookup for non-registered commenters**: This will pull avatars from Gravatar.com - Your choice. The same rules apply if the avatar is inappropriate for your site, then you may wish to disable this.

▶ **Enable reCaptcha**: This is an anti-spam feature. You'll need to sign up for reCaptcha to use this.

▶ Further down (not shown in the preceding screenshot) you will find a section in **Parameters** called: **Content Cleanup Settings**. In that section, there are two important settings for stripping out HTML tags. I suggest as a matter of course that you enable this to prevent malicious code from being added to comments.

There are many more **Parameter** settings available that control Twitter feeds, and one to integrate Google search on your site.

Take a few minutes to review all the **Parameter** settings and adjust them to your needs.

Moderating content

Now you have comments enabled by category or item and you have configured your comments parameters. Once your site is live and you start receiving comments, you'll need to moderate them.

1. Open K2 Dashboard.

2. Click **Comments**.

3. There you will see the comments left on your site. Here is a partial example:

There are several fields that span across this comment. My options for this article are:

▶ **Edit**

▶ **Publish**

▶ **Unpublish**

▶ **Delete**

Or I could even delete all the unpublished comments.

Editing a comment.

You may wish to edit a comment for many reasons such as misspellings or trademark violations. Doing so is simple. Click **Edit** under the comment. This will open the comment as follows:

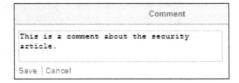

Once I am satisfied, I can publish, and I am done.

This works the same for all comments on your site.

K2 does not provide any mechanism to alert you when you receive comments. You may wish to look into third-party extensions that will provide notification of pending comments for your K2 articles. One such extension that will give you this functionality is `http://www.jiliko.net/en/Resources/Extensions/K2/K2-Multi-Notify`.

Summary

In this chapter we scratched the surface of K2 by learning how to install, configure, and set up categories. We also explored how to set up a master category enabling you to take advantage of the inheritance features.

K2 offers some great features such as extra fields and tags to improve both the usability of your site and the search engine optimization.

Using the built-in commenting system in K2, you can enable users to leave comments on content.

Overall, K2 is a good Content Construction Kit to have in your design tool bag.

8
Installing Third-party Extensions

In this chapter, we will cover:

- ▸ Installation and configuration of eXtplorer
- ▸ Content upload extension
- ▸ Installation and configuration of jomCalendar extension
- ▸ CompojoomComment system for Joomla!

Introduction

Joomla! is an extensible framework, which means, developers can add to it. In fact there is a very healthy ecosystem of both paid and free third-party extensions. This chapter will take you through installation, configuration, and use of some selected extensions. Most of these are commercially available extensions. The choice of inclusion of some commercial extensions is based on the differences in support models and their usefulness to a successful Joomla! site.

You can find most extensions free and commercial at `extensions.Joomla.org`.

The reader is advised to backup your site and database completely before installing any third-party extensions of any kind. This is a good practice to get into and will help you recover quickly should there be any type of trouble.

Installing and using eXtplorer

eXtplorer is a nice add-on for using the functions of FTP from within your Joomla! site. This feature-rich, free extension is easy to install and use.

eXtplorer includes the ability to:

- Browse directories and files
- Edit, copy, move, and delete files
- Search, upload, and download files
- Create new files and directories
- Create and extract archives with files and directories
- Changing file permissions (also known as chmod)

Getting ready

- Download a copy of eXtplorer from the following website: `http://joomlacode.org/gf/project/joomlaxplorer/frs/`
- Install using the **Components | Install / Uninstall**

How to do it...

Now that you have installed the eXtplorer, you're ready to see how it works.

1. Navigate to **Components | eXtplorer** and click it to open. You'll see this screen:

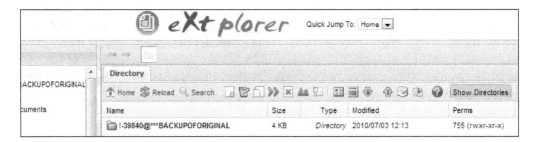

This is the primary screen for eXtplorer. Let's get familiar with the various sections of this component before learning how to use them.

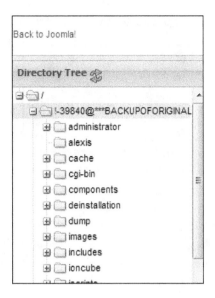

This is the directory tree of the machine you're using. This would be your desktop in most cases. Keep in mind, that wherever you log in to your site from, this left part of the screen is the local machine.

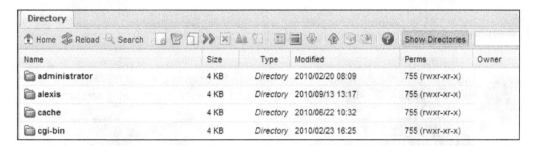

This screenshot represents your website folders.

This portion of the screen is the main control icons for eXtplorer. You can issue all the commands from here.

If you right-click on any file or directory, you'll see this pop-up toolbar:

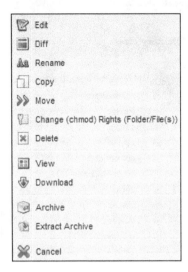

These are a subset of the toolbar functions.

Looking towards the upper right-hand corner, you'll see a small menu item that looks as follows:

Current mode: extplorer [Logout]. You could switch to ftp mode.

2. This extension is a collection of tools that can be used in place of a FTP client, such as FileZilla. Clicking the **ftp mode** button will open the following screen:

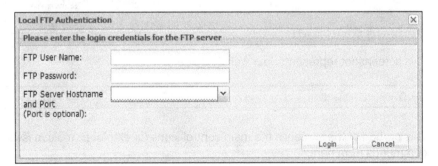

This will prompt you to put in your FTP credentials. You likely will not need this.

Now that we have had a basic look, let's drive through this component and conduct a few basic activities.

Create a new file or directory

1. On the right-hand screen, look at the toolbar for this component:

2. Click the prompt to get this box:

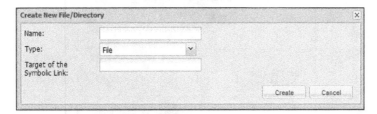

3. To use this put in the **Name** for your file or directory.

4. Pull down the drop-down menu and select **File** or **Directory**. Ignore **Target of the Symbolic Link** for the purposes of this recipe.

5. Click **Create**.

Changing permissions

Lots of issues in Joomla! are caused by setting the incorrect permissions on files and folders. The rule is files should be set to **644** and folders set to **755**.

Looking at the screen on the right in eXtplorer, you'll see a column labeled **Perms**. Let's set permissions for our newly created file from the last step.

1. Right-click the file you just created. Here's mine:

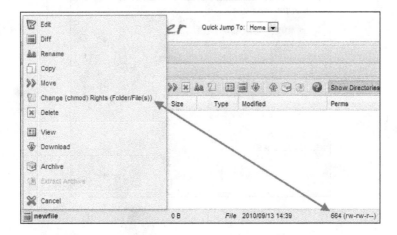

2. The right-click on the file called **newfile** brings up this menu. I have pointed the arrow at the control and at the permissions. You see the permissions for the file are 664. It should be set for 644.

3. Choose **Change (chmod) Rights (Folder/Files(s))**.

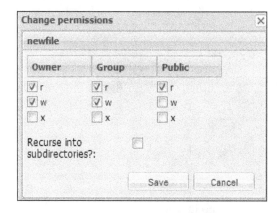

4. In this case, we want to remove the write (**w**) permissions from the **Group**.

5. Uncheck the (**w**) in the preceding group and click **Save**.

6. Now you will see the **newfile** file has the correct permissions.

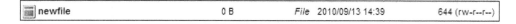

If you wanted to change the permission of a directory, and all the subdirectories in it, you would follow the same steps above but, you would need to do two different steps.

Check the blocks as follows for directories and check the box that says **Recurse into subdirectories?:** Then click **Save**.

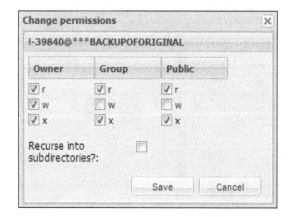

These settings translate to 755, meaning you (as the **Owner**) can read, write, and execute or run the file. The **Group** and **Public** can only read and execute. They cannot make any changes.

Uploading and downloading files:

On the toolbar, locate these two buttons:

How it works...

eXtplorer offers up several key tools all built into a Joomla! extension. The extension can handle most of the server-side needs such as the ones shown here and a few more.

This extension works with the native functions such as `chmod` and `TAR` to take care of the day-to-day tasks.

Using and configuring content uploader extension

Joomla! allows you to manage your content from an easy-to-use interface and present your content to your visitors in the form of your website.

Managing your content is easy when you have a small number of pages, or articles you wish to present. However, when you face dozens or hundreds of pieces of information, that must be manually inserted - then you have a large task on your hands. Today people manage vast quantities of data using spreadsheets, using this free extension you can upload and create articles automatically. This will work with Excel and OpenOffice and other formats. As an example, say you have 15 rows of spreadsheet data; with this tool, you can create 15 articles - automatically.

In this recipe, we'll take a detailed look at this extension.

This extension is available free at `www.freakedout.de/Joomla!extensions/`

Getting ready

▸ Visit and register for free at `http://www.freakedout.de` and download the free content uploader

▸ Download test spreadsheet `www.freakedout.de/media/Shop_sample.xls`

▸ Upload and install using **Extensions | Install / Uninstall**

How to do it...

To demonstrate, we'll assume that your content is entered row by row into a spreadsheet. Using the provided sample, which provides a simple to understand scenario for you, we'll work through the use of this extension. Let's assume you want to create articles with information about books you have on sale. This example will create five articles about books, which will include information like author, title of the book, its rating, the price, whether it is in stock or not, a description and other information related to the book.

For this example it is essential to know where you want each column to appear and what row your data starts at. The following screenshot shows what the sample sheet looks like. For your own purposes name your columns however way you would like.

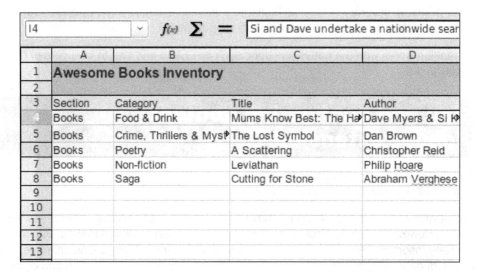

The extension will follow a few Joomla! conventions, namely categories and sections. In this example, we want to upload the articles into the section called **Books**. The category of the books will depend on the individual book. The sections and categories are automatically created based on the spreadsheet data. To assist the site visitors in locating the book of their choice, the article **Title** will be the same as the Title. Here is the example:

ch for Britain's lost recipes - those forgotten gems or secret scribbles handed d

	E	F	G	H	I	J	
	Rating	RRP	Price	InStock?	Description	Meta1	
	4,7	£15,00	£10,00	16 February 2010	Si and Dave undertake a n	metastuff	
	1,5	£15,00	£9,00	In Stock.	--Barry Forshaw	metastuff	
	3	£10,00	£7,19	Temporarily out o	Lucinda Gane, Christopher	metastuff	
	4	£8,00	£5,79	In Stock.	The story of a man's obses	metastuff	
	5	£5,00	£3,86	In Stock.	centre.	metastuff	

The sample spreadsheet contains information such as the book **Rating, RRP, Price, Availability**, and **Description**. This will all become an article. Please note, you can predefine every setting for your content articles from within the spreadsheet.

Uploading your articles:

1. Click **Components | Content Uploader**.

2. Choose **Upload Articles**:

3. Click **Browse...** and locate the sample spreadsheet.

4. Click **Upload** in upper right-corner.

5. You should receive a message that your upload was successful.

6. Click **Content | Article Manager**.

   Here you can see the various articles created by the spreadsheet. If you want to publish, unpublish, and so on. You can do so now

How it works...

This extension works using the underlying code in Joomla! to create an article or articles out of a spreadsheet. The steps to create it are identical to it as if you created the article by hand.

This is a great way to get lots of content up on your site in a short period of time. In this example, we uploaded books, yet that could be anything you wish to upload.

There's more...

The **Content Uploader** - is a simple and easy-to-use tool. Start by clicking **Components | Content Uploader** to use the extension.

This is the section of the screen we'll be reviewing:

Steps:

▸ **First Data Row** indicates the starting point in your spreadsheet. In this example, we set it for **4**. This is the default one. You will need to choose the starting row for your data accordingly.

▸ Column **C** is in this example the book's **Title**. We want our articles to have the same title as the book. For your production data, you would of course set the title **Column** to be whatever you want.

▸ Column **A** is the **Section** for Joomla!

▸ Column **B** is the **Category** for Joomla!

The primary settings for each article are now set, but we still have all the information pertaining to each book that we somehow need to get into each article.

For the sample we have a two-column table with the title of the field in the second column inside the first column.

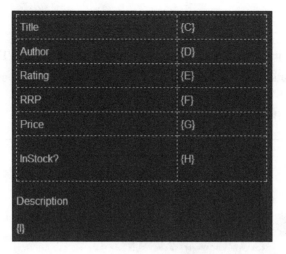

When entering column reference inside your WYSIWYG editor you have to make sure to use curly brackets around your reference - **{C}** - for example. This way the content uploader knows to differentiate between regular text and data that is to be pulled out of the spreadsheet.

▶ Click **Save** in the **Manage Configurations** section to **Save** your preferences.

jomCalendar

While we are awash in calendars in both the Joomla! world and in normal life, this extension will help keep you on track. This recipe discusses jomCalendar from `COREPHP.COM`. It is a commercial extension and was chosen for inclusion due to its great feature-set and support options.

`JomCalender` allows you to have multiple calendars to track anything you wish. Examples include birthdays, sporting events, work calendar, religious holidays, or more.

Getting ready

To use the calendar, you will need to purchase it. You will need your administrator login for installation.

How to do it...

1. Login as Admin and install using **Extension Manager | Install/Uninstall**.

2. Once installation is done you will see a warning about the themes for the calendar. This won't affect our recipe.

3. Click **Install The Sample Data** button.

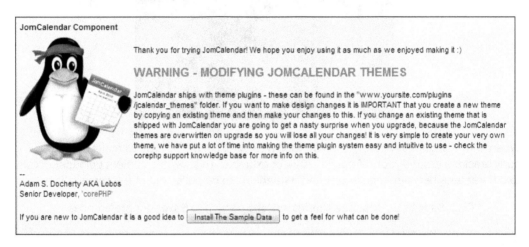

You'll receive a warning. As this is the first run through, we are not concerned about this. You should, however, keep this in mind upon upgrading as you will lose data.

4. Click **OK** to install sample data.

5. Click **Extensions | JomCalender | Calendar**.

Here we'll 'add' a calendar to the sample data.

6. Scroll down to the lower left where you see the sample calendars

7. Click **New**.

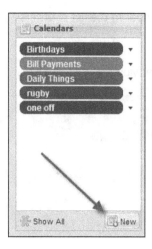

This will bring up the following dialog box. This one is filled out for you.

8. Fill in **Name** and **Description**.
9. Choose the Calendar color and click **Save**.

We now have added a "work" calendar to the list of others.

Adding events:

1. Right-click on the calendar view.

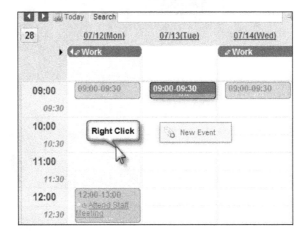

2. Click the **New Event** pop-up that shows.

3. Fill in this dialog box with your appointment information. Don't forget to change the calendar it belongs to.

4. Click **Save**.

You now have a new event in your work calendar.

How it works...

jomCalendar takes the concept of calendar to a whole new level through the use of the multilevel, multiview.

As this is a component, you can add it to the front end of your site like any other extension. Assigning it a menu item allows you to provide visitors a calendar on your site.

There's more...

The jomCalendar is capable of quite a bit. Here are a few other nuggets.

jomCalendar as a menu item

1. Click **Menus | Main Menu** (or whatever menu you want).
2. Add **New Menu Item**.
3. Select **jomCalendar** as your menu item.
4. You'll now need to choose your "view".

There are several views we can choose from. In this instance, I chose **Timeline View**.

5. Give it a title (publicly viewable).
6. Give it an alias.
7. On the upper right-hand side - choose your calendar (I am choosing **rugby**).

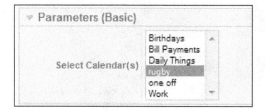

8. Click **Save** and then preview site.

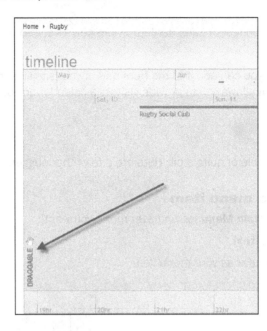

The menu item on our site (**Rugby Calendar**) shows a 'timeline' mode of the **Rugby Social Club**. The arrow you may note, is pointing to draggable. This means you can use your mouse to drag the calendar back and forth in time.

Displaying two or more calendars on your site

We have a calendar on our site, showing the Rugby Social Club calendar. What if we wanted a 'work' calendar for our members? Let's add another jomCalendar.

1. Click **Menus | Main Menu** (or whatever menu you want).

2. Add new menu item.

3. Select **jomCalendar** as your menu item.

4. You'll now need to choose your "view".

5. Select the **Work** calendar.

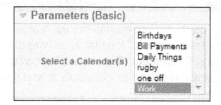

6. Click **Save** and then preview site.

    Here are the two menu items showing the calendar.

7. Clicking on the **Work Calendar** shows us a very different view from the previous **Rugby Social Club Calendar**:

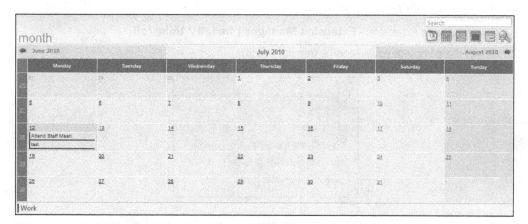

    Keeping in mind that this calendar can have multiple views, multiple calendars can be made private or public.

    It is a powerful calendar extension for your Joomla! site.

Using and configuring CompojoomComment

When you surf the web these days, you see comments everywhere. Comments on news, on YouTube videos, newspaper sites and more. Joomla! in its core does not offer a powerful commenting system for visitors. **CompojoomComment** allows you the ability to offer commenting capability on nearly any article or extension. It works with third-party components such as K2, DocMan, and others.

In this recipe you will learn to install, configure, and use this "must have" extension. You may download a copy of this from the PacktPub website. Support subscriptions are available from http://www.compojoom.com.

Getting ready

Please download this extension from PacktPub or the developer's site to try this exercise.

How to do it...

1. Login to your Administrator Console.

2. Install the extension - **Extension Manager | Install / Uninstall**.

3. Once complete you'll receive this message.

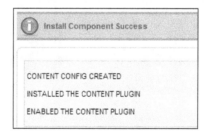

4. Preview the front end of your site and your content (all of it) will be comment-enabled as follows:

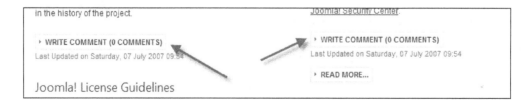

As you see I have two articles in this picture that are now 'enabled' for comments.

5. Clicking on the **WRITE COMMENT(0 COMMENTS)** gives the visitor this:

How it works...

CompojoomComment works by adding itself to any and all content items you choose. It works by taking advantage of the Joomla! plugin system - allowing added functionality to your Joomla! site.

When users post their comments, they will either be moderated or displayed automatically, depending on your settings.

As it does allow commenting on basically everything, it also offers you the ability to exclude specific extensions or articles or categories or sections.

In the following section, you'll learn about configuring it for your site.

There's more...

CompojoomComment can be configured and tweaked to specify exactly what you wish to be commented on.

Configuring CompojoomComment

1. Login as administrator.

2. Navigate to **Components | Compojoom |Settings**.

3. Once in settings click **com_content**.

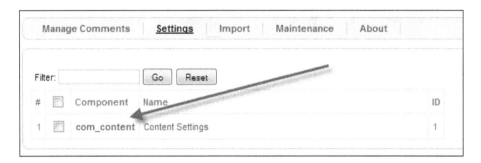

You'll be presented with a lot of options - let's break them down in the following screens.

Most of your settings will be controlled from these boxes:

▶ **General**: Handles a large number of functions such as what sections/categories or extensions to include.

▶ **Security**: It deals directly with spam, banned IP's, registered users, profanity, or other banned words and more.

▶ **Posting**: It gives you a great deal of control over how postings themselves are handled.

▶ **Layout**: It governs the look and feel of the screens.

▶ **Integrations**: It enables integration with various third-party applications.

Let's look in more detail at the first tab - **General**.

This portion of the screen is where you can 'include' or 'exclude' various parts of your site from being comment enabled.

- ▶ **Exclude/Include**: This radio button dictates the behavior of the rest of this screen. If you set it for **Exclude** - which is default - then anything you check in the sections or categories will be 'excluded' from having comments. And as you can imagine, the opposite is true. If you select the radio button **Include**, then only the content you check will be allowed to have comments added.

- ▶ **Exclude/Include Item Ids**: This will exclude or include various item IDs. These can be an article, an extension or any other resource available to Joomla!

- ▶ **Disable additional comments**: Disables the comment form for the specified content id.

- ▶ **Exclude/Include Sections, Categories**: This will exclude or include various sections (which can affect categories) and/or categories.

  Once you make your selections - click **Save**.

Managing comments

You have the ability to moderate comments on your site. Meaning, you may not want to let just anyone post comments to your site without some checks and balances. The number of times that you want to moderate will be based on your own policies.

To moderate you would follow these steps:

1. Login as Admin.

2. Select **Components | CompojoomComment | Manage Comments**.

3. Once in there, you will see all the comments ready for approval or rejection.

This screen will show all comments and allow you to edit, unpublish, publish, or delete.

In this instance, we want to delete John Doe's posting (the third one marked in the screenshot) so we check it and click **Delete** in the upper right-hand side.

If we select one and click the writer's name, this is how it looks:

You can edit to your heart's desire. If it's an abusive poster, you can capture the IP from this screen and ban them in the **Security** tab.

After you edit - be sure and save.

With CompojoomComment you can manage and edit the postings from the front end by logging in with proper permissions as well.

Summary

Joomla! has a very healthy developer ecosystem providing both commercially available and free extensions. Commercial extensions are usually offered on a per site or on a club basis.

In this chapter we looked at a number of useful extensions that can add a great deal of functionality to your site. The content uploader allows the ability to bring in vast amounts of data from a spreadsheet into your site, automatically creating articles.

Working with eXtplorer you have the built-in power of FTP and some server-side commands such as changing permissions and archiving.

Adding the powerful jomCalendar to your site gives you the feature-rich. multi-calendar system for such site applications as sports teams or social events.

And last but not least, a commenting application that gives you instant comment capability across a range of resources.

The extensions in `Joomla.org` site is filled with many wonderful extensions in several categories. Take some time and browse through it for ideas and extensions to improve your site.

9
Troubleshooting

In this chapter, we will cover:

- ▶ Developing a troubleshooting methodology
- ▶ Trouble connecting to a database
- ▶ Trouble installing or reinstalling an extension
- ▶ SSH and FTP connection issues

Introduction

Troubleshooting is a simple matter of following a process. In fact, I believe that anyone can learn the basic troubleshooting skills needed for the successful care and feeding of their website.

This short chapter ties together many things that have been covered in this book. Several trouble spots have been covered in the various chapters and now you will gain a methodology to apply those various solutions to your problem. The key topic in this chapter is for you to learn how to troubleshoot your Joomla! installation.

When system trouble occurs, many people panic, freeze, or start turning things on and off with no methodology. In the computer services industry, this is known as "shotgunning" or in other words, throwing every possible solution at it at once.

I've seen situations where someone will ask you to assist, and in the meantime, they ask someone else to as well. What happens is you're both in the website, and do not know it. Talk about a mess!

In this chapter, the first recipe will be to help you gain a basic idea about troubleshooting. Then, we'll look at some common situations that you may run into.

Developing a 'troubleshooting mentality'

Troubleshooting is very much like baking a cake. You can read the instructions, that is, follow the process and your cake will likely come out of the oven and taste and look great.

You can ignore the instructions and the best case is your cake, may taste ok, but won't look right and the texture will be poor. In other words, you won't reach your goal of having a nice cake to serve.

Troubleshooting Joomla! or any other computer system is a matter of separating the symptoms from the facts of the situation by following a process.

Often at times, when you are troubleshooting an issue, it's easy to accept the symptom as the problem, running off to treat it, rather than discover what caused it.

What I mean by that is, often at times a symptom is just that - a symptom. The root cause is what you are after. Resist the urge to accept the first thing you think is wrong as the final answer and not look further.

In this case, let's create a fantasy situation where a site has been hacked. The conventional (and often correct) wisdom is that you have an extension that is vulnerable, permissions wrong or weak passwords. And while those are true and frequent, you need to look at all systems involved and take the necessary steps such as patching and updating to ensure you are safe again.

Let's dive in using the hacked site as an example of troubleshooting.

How to do it...

The situation presented here is that your website has been hacked. You clean up the hack, and the hacker returns, again and again. You cannot locate how they are getting in.

Your configuration is as follows:

▶ You are on a Shared host, running PHP 5.2.0-8; it has the Apache webserver and MySQL Database server

▶ Joomla! 1.5.14

▶ Several extensions, some out of date, and vulnerable.

Right now, the obvious problem that could be misdiagnosed is assuming that the version of Joomla! is the problem.

The correct way to look at this situation is that it's one possibility. The version of Joomla! is out of date and could be the source of the attack.

1. Step one is to update your Joomla! to the latest version of 1.5. Double check that your permissions on your site are correct by making sure that the directories are 755 and the files are 644.

2. The next item in our troubleshooting arsenal is to make an offline copy of the log files. This would include all logs, access, error logs, and FTP logs. We'll need these shortly.

3. Make a backup if you don't have a recently known good backup. This will at least preserve the site as it is even if that means it's hacked.

4. Many times a hacker's aim is to put some kind of backdoor, Trojan horse or virus on to your site. Scan the files locally (using your desktop) with a good virus scanner.

5. As we updated our Joomla! site first, this, many times, will restore a hacked site. This is of course very dependent on the type of attack. However, in our example it was part of the scenario to update.

6. Review the extensions and update that are out of date. Remove the ones not in use. Check to see if the site is still hacked. If so, then you'll need to track down the damage. In this case however, we'll assume for the story, that the site is clean.

7. The last step is to make a fresh backup and copy it offline.

   After all that you come to work the next day and find that you've been hacked again!

   Now the troubleshooting begins:

▶ Ensure that your file permissions are set globally to 644.

▶ Ensure directory permissions are set globally to 755.

▶ Eliminate any viruses that are present. Many things like C99 control programs are very common in hacks. They are not considered as traditional viruses, however, are quite damaging. This is done by locating them with your virus scanning methods as mentioned previously. Other areas to consider are the template files. Many times they can get code embedded in them, which may be notorious. Look carefully and see if the date / time stamp has recently changed. Edit the file and remove any included code that should not be there.

▶ If you had viruses, and removed them, then the site is free from viruses. Recheck that a new vulnerability has not been discovered in your current version of Joomla! and recheck to make sure all the extensions are up to date.

   In this example, we eliminated the website as the source by ensuring we updated our site and extensions and removed any malware. Additionally all the damage was repaired.

   As you know, your website is made up of many applications and systems. A brief list would contain the following:

▶ The core Joomla! and third-party extensions

▶ FTP or SFTP system

▶ Mail server

▶ Apache or IIS (Microsoft)

▶ MySQL

▶ The operating system(Linux or Microsoft)

▶ Various supporting components both on the machine and in the network

Working through that list - we need to check each one off to locate the real cause. We have eliminated Joomla! and extensions as the case by updating and cleaning the viruses off.

1. Create a small PHP file and name it PHPINFO.PHP and place it on your site. Using your text editor add this to the file.

   ```php
   <?php
   phpinfo();
   ?>
   ```

2. Upload this file to your site's root directory, set permission to 644 and visit your site as follows:

   ```
   http://www.domain.com/phpinfo.php
   ```

   Doing so will bring up all the environmental information about your site. Here's the first part of the screen:

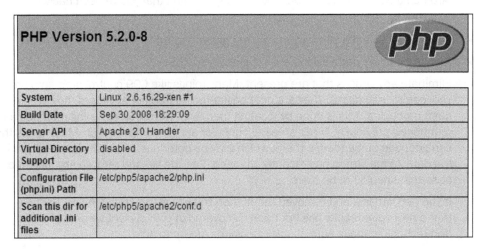

PHP Version 5.2.0-8	
System	Linux 2.6.16.29-xen #1
Build Date	Sep 30 2008 18:29:09
Server API	Apache 2.0 Handler
Virtual Directory Support	disabled
Configuration File (php.ini) Path	/etc/php5/apache2/php.ini
Scan this dir for additional .ini files	/etc/php5/apache2/conf.d

3. Note your PHP version.

4. Scroll down to till you see the Apache section:

Apache Environment

Variable	Value
HTTP_HOST	test.
HTTP_USER_AGENT	Mozilla/5.0 (Windows; U; Windows NT 6.1; en-US; rv:1.9.2.9) Gecko/20100824 Firefox/3.6.9
HTTP_ACCEPT	text/html,application/xhtml+xml,application/xml;q=0.9,*/*;q=0.8
HTTP_ACCEPT_LANGUAGE	en-us,en;q=0.5
HTTP_ACCEPT_ENCODING	gzip,deflate
HTTP_ACCEPT_CHARSET	ISO-8859-1,utf-8;q=0.7,*;q=0.7
HTTP_KEEP_ALIVE	115
HTTP_CONNECTION	keep-alive
HTTP_REFERER	
PATH	/usr/local/bin:/usr/bin:/bin
SERVER_SIGNATURE	<address>Apache/2.2.3 (Debian) DAV/2 mod_python/3.2.10 Python/2.4.4 PHP/5.2.0-8· Server at test. Port 80</address>

The arrow shows us the Apache version (in this case version 2.2.3 and it is out of date).

Additionally, we see the Operating Systems is Debian linux and a few other important data points.

5. Repeat this by locating the MySQL version in this same manner.

Once we have all that, we can check to see if they are the most current versions. In the event of this Apache environment, we would want our host to update the Apache.

Let's assume however, we have eliminated this server's software components as they are all up-to-date.

> You'll want to remove the `phpinfo.php` file from your site as soon as you are done with it. This could provide valuable information to an attacker.

We return to the scene of the crime once again and review the site, but this time we pay particular attention to the log files. We see a lot of activity, but you have a busy site and that's expected.

Looking at the "**date and time**" stamp of the altered files tells us that last night; the sites files were changed at **4:24 AM**. Making a note of that, it gives us a starting time to look for the trouble.

Looking in the Apache Logs, we do not see any activity at that time. It must be somewhere else.

Troubleshooting

Next we'll check the FTP logs. Doing so you note activity around that time.

You see:

```
1.10.20.30  JSmith108 [23/Jul/2010:04:23:44 -0500] "STOR exp_
ingom0wnar.c"
1.10.20.30  JSmith108 [23/Jul/2010:04:23:44 -0500] "STOR pwnkernel.c"
226 764
1.10.20.30  JSmith108 [23/Jul/2010:04:23:45 -0500] "STOR exp_
cheddarbay.c"
1.10.20.30  JSmith108 [23/Jul/2010:04:23:46 -0500] "STOR exp_
wunderbar.c"
1.10.20.30  JSmith108 [23/Jul/2010:04:23:47 -0500] "STOR exp_
therebel.c"
1.10.20.30  JSmith108 [23/Jul/2010:04:23:48 -0500] "STOR exp_
moosecox.c"
1.10.20.30  JSmith108 [23/Jul/2010:04:23:48 -0500] "STOR exp_vmware.c"
1.10.20.30  JSmith108 [23/Jul/2010:04:23:49 -0500] "STOR exp_
framework.h" 226
1.10.20.30  JSmith108 [23/Jul/2010:04:23:49 -0500] "STOR run_null_
exploits.sh"
1.10.20.30  JSmith108 [23/Jul/2010:04:23:50 -0500] "STOR run_nonnull_
exploits.sh"
1.10.20.30  JSmith108 [23/Jul/2010:04:23:51 -0500] "STOR exp_
paokara.c" 226
1.10.20.30  JSmith108 [23/Jul/2010:04:23:56 -0500] "STOR exploit.c"
226 44438
1.10.20.30  JSmith108 [23/Jul/2010:04:23:56 -0500] "STOR funny.jpg"
226 67332
1.10.20.30  JSmith108 [23/Jul/2010:04:23:57 -0500] "STOR exp_
powerglove.c"
1.10.20.30  JSmith108 [23/Jul/2010:04:23:57 -0500] "CWD /YourWebSite.
com"
1.10.20.30  JSmith108 [23/Jul/2010:04:23:37 -0500] "STOR run_null_
exploits.sh"
```

 This is a real FTP log taken from an attacked site. It has been edited to protect the attacked site and to remove specific information not needed for our purposes.

You see many files have been uploaded using your user ID. This indicates that someone has your FTP password and has uploaded some strange files. You change your FTP password, as apparently they got in through your FTP ID of JSmith108.

You come in on day three and the hack is back. At this point, you need to look at the parts of the system. Meaning, all the parts that make up your site. This includes any desktops you use to connect.

It is time to scan your desktop and eliminate that as the source - you might have a key logger which can record every key stroke and report those to an attacker. This scenario actually plays out very often. Don't take chances get a good and reputable virus scanner and keep it up to date. Scan your desktop or notebook at a minimum weekly.

But I'm running a Macintosh..

Please don't fall into the trap that Mac's do not get viruses. They can and do. In fact, any computing device that talks to any other devices (including digital photo frames) can get a virus.

Scanning the desktop concludes you have a trojan horse on your site. They have been watching your every mouse click, grabbing your FTP, banking and any other passwords. This is how they were able to continuously get in, you changed your password and they simply got it from the key logger on the machine.

The point of this scenario is to show you that if you follow and stay on the path of it must be "X" and do not consider your website as a whole, including other computers, then you are wasting your time.

One interesting point about the attack that was just shown is this particular code that the hacker was uploading is made to evade some special Linux OS security measures.

How it works...

Troubleshooting is a process - Here are some questions that you can ask as you troubleshoot to get you going.

- What is the EXACT problem? - This does not mean 'it's broken' or 'it's not working'. This means something like "When I click on this menu item, I get a 404 error. When I click on the other menu item I get a Server Error 500.' Knowing the exact problem or symptom will help you get the help you need.

- What the problem isn't. - This may sound dumb, but think about it. If your Joomla! site comes UP, but specific components fail such as a menu item or an extension then most likely it isn't any of the following:
  - The server: We know this because the site does work.
  - Joomla! version: While this could be the case, a quick update or refresh of the Joomla! core files would eliminate it.
  - Apache: If the website did not come up at all, then Apache is a good place to look at, but if specific parts fail, it is less likely it's Apache.
  - MySQL: The database has to be running if any of the site comes up.

In this case, it leaves the version of PHP, your browser, or its settings, or the extension. It could be something simple like a search engine-friendly extension that has malfunctioned. The point is to eliminate (deduce) what is working and set that aside.

▶ What has changed?: Be honest, ask a lot of questions. If you are the only one working on your site and you know for sure you haven't changed anything then start looking elsewhere. Here are some questions to ask to help you figure out what has changed:

  ❑ Has the host upgraded some part of the server?

  ❑ If they did, what was it? Is it compatible with my software? - Examples include, (at time of writing) older versions of PHP 5.x.x have troubles with some of the latest versions of Joomla! 1.5.

  ❑ If something has changed, but host is not responsible, then who did? Have you been hacked? Did somebody 'assist' you such as a co-worker?

▶ If you updated an extension or Joomla!, does putting the older version back make the problem go away? If so - then that's a good piece to the puzzle. Try to determine if that extension works on other sites. If it does, then start looking back at your server and your site. Is there a conflict with it? Does it have a dependency?

▶ Can the problem be replicated? In other words, if you find a bug in Joomla!, can you tell the developers of Joomla! how to repeat the steps? If not then, they may not be able to duplicate it and thus fix it.

Your objective in troubleshooting is to isolate the root cause of the issue and resolve it. Once you do, the problem should go away.

Some tips for successful troubleshooting are keeping a clear head and not letting the presence of a problem confuse you. Problems happen; they are simply puzzles to be solved.

Don't try to do everything at once. In other words, if the symptom presented could be caused by more than one thing, do not change a several things at once.

Change the most probable solution first, and then move to the less probable.

What's most probable?

The most probable root cause is not often easy to determine, but using the preceding questions as a guide is a great start. I like to seek out the root cause in this order:

▶ What has changed?

▶ When was it changed?

▶ Did the problem occur before the change?

▶ Who has access to the site (besides you...)?

▶ What has been done to fix it?

In a nutshell, troubleshooting is matter of eliminating the obvious, looking at what's left, no matter how improbable it may be. Always consider a website a holistic system involving a server, the website, extensions on the site, users (who may have changed something), the host, and your own systems that connect to it.

There's more...

Now that you have an idea of how it works, let's break down a few common systems in Joomla! and see how they troubleshoot them.

Unable to connect to database

Occasionally things happen to the database or settings. The first thing you want to do is to check to see if the database itself is running. If you can reach it with your control panel or `phpMyadmin`, then the database is likely running. If not, then contact the host.

The next item to check is the `configuration.php` file. Within that file, located in the root of Joomla! are the settings for the database. Joomla! will look there to connect to the database.

Steps to check:

1. Make sure that the file **configuration.php** exists.
2. If it exists open it and look for these lines:

   var $dbtype = 'mysql';
   var $password ='password goes here'
   var $host = 'localhost';
   var $user = 'myuser_2020';
   var $db = 'mydb_2010';
   var $dbprefix = 'jos_';

   Your information will vary from that above. These five lines are the lines that tell Joomla! what it needs to know to connect to the database.

   ▶ `var $dbtype` is the type of database. In 99% of the cases, this will be MySQL. If you are unsure - check with your host.

   ▶ `var $password` is the password that is set for the user of that database.

   ▶ `var $host` is 'typically' `localhost`. [However, in the case of GoDaddy®, it can be a long host name.] *Your host has full discretion over the database server name. Placing a quick call to your host will answer this question.*

   ▶ `var $user` is the database username that connects to the instance of the database.

   ▶ `var $db` is the name you gave the specific database when you created it.

   ▶ `var $dbprefix` = unless you change this, this will be `jos_`. You can make it whatever you want (at time of installation of Joomla!)

Check these settings against what you set up the database with. If they are wrong or missing something. Joomla! will not connect. If they are correct and the Database is running, then you will need to seek out other potential causes.

Inability to reinstall an extension

Occasionally, when you update an extension, even if you remove it, you have trouble getting it reinstalled. You may get an error indicating, it's still there. Another error is if you lose an extension folder - say by accidental deletion.

All these can be fixed very simply:

▸ First check the file and directory permissions. If the directories are not writable, then an extension will not install. Remember directory permissions are 755.

▸ Check to see if the extension folder(s) (in the `/modules` or `/components` directories) exist, then rename it. Try installing again.

▸ If that fails, be sure you renamed both the `administrator/module` and `/components` folders. If they do not exist or you renamed them, move to the next step.

▸ Log in to your database.

▸ Make a back up.

▸ Locate the appropriate table, look in the MODULES tables for modules, and components tables for components. Once in there - delete it.

 This is an advanced method. Do not do this if you are unsure about how to restore a database.

▸ Now that you have removed any traces of the extension from the database attempt reinstall.

SSH related issues.

SecureShell or **SSH** is my preferred means to connect to a webserver. It is inherently safer than FTP is. There are several methods to set up an SSH connection on a server and depending on the configuration, there could be several things to check. Let's review a basic SSH configuration.

The server must:

▸ Support SecureShell

▸ Your host most likely must set up your access

▸ You will need a host name or IP for the server, username, and password

Optionally:

- ▸ You may need an 'alternate' port number
- ▸ You may need a Public, Private key setup - meaning you have to have a digitally encrypted key on your desktop to submit to the host when you log in.
- ▸ Possibly other security measure may be in place - very host dependent such as including specific IP's that are allowed in.

If you cannot get into a SSH setup, here are a few steps and questions.

- ▸ Has your host set up your account to allow it?
- ▸ Do you have the right username and password?
- ▸ Do you have the right host name/IP address?
- ▸ Does your host require your IP to be whitelisted?
- ▸ If you could previously get on - has your IP address changed?
- ▸ Ask the host to check and make sure your IP isn't blacklisted.
- ▸ Have you setup a private key on your machine? (advanced)

If you go through these steps, you will likely be able to get in quickly.

Ownership of files and directories

Another issue that sometimes occurs is if you upload a file or files via SSH and your permissions are either higher or different than the web *users*.

You upload a file or files to a website and it fails to work.

Again, going through your troubleshooting steps -such as - what has changed? will lead you quickly to answer, "new files". Assuming the new files are known to work, you may need to have your host change permissions and ownership of the files to the same user that is attached to your webserver.

This can be the Apache user, the `NOBOBY` user or whatever the host set up as the user that runs (internally) the webserver.

If you FTP in and see `ROOT | ROOT` as the owner, it's a good chance that the files will not work.

The summary is, if you upload, and something doesn't work out of the box, be sure and check the ownership and permissions of the files.

FTP troubleshooting

Most users will use FTP as their preferred means to upload and download files to their website. Troubleshooting this connection is no different than an SSH connection. However, some things differ in the traditional FTP application from SSH.

You will not have a private or public key. Chances are the port it connects to has not changed, as SSH can. This means uploads with the wrong permissions and ownership of files is not a problem. Having said that, here are a few things that could go wrong with FTP.

- No FTP username setup or you have the wrong one
- Password is wrong
- Host (or someone) has set up FTP to go to a blank folder
- You have binary mode set up on your FTP client and it should be ASCII mode. Or vice-versa

Most of the time, an FTP hostname looks like this:

`ftp.Mydomain.com`

The user name can vary, but often will resemble this:

`myuser@mydomain.com`

There usually is very little that can go wrong with FTP. It is highly reliable for this type of connection.

Summary

Troubleshooting is many times a matter of common sense and patience. You may not be a super technical person, but you can easily follow the steps outlined above for troubleshooting.

When you find yourself with a broken site, remain calm. Writing everything down helps.

In this chapter, you learned how to pull apart a problem to get to the root cause. You now have some important questions that will quickly help you reach that point.

Some common issues that happen to Joomla! sites occasionally wrapped up our chapter.

Happy troubleshooting!

10
Securing your Joomla! Site

In this chapter, we will cover:

- ▸ Setting permissions for your site
- ▸ Patching
- ▸ Using `.htaccess` to protect your site
- ▸ Preventing unauthorized directory viewing
- ▸ Adding a universal error page
- ▸ Turning off your server's "banner"
- ▸ Blocking IP's and evil bots
- ▸ `php.ini` settings for security

Introduction

Joomla! is a well known and popular platform. In fact, the `joomla.org` site itself receives several thousand hits a year. While there isn't a known figure for the amount of websites running Joomla!, a search in Google revealed over ten million sites that have it or reference it.

> allinurl: joomla
> About 10,200,000 results (0.29 seconds)

With a popular platform like Joomla!, sites are a target for hackers. And many of these sites are easy targets for a variety of reasons such as incorrect permissions, sites not being properly maintained, bad hosting choices, and more.

In this chapter you'll learn how to do the easy and medium difficulty tasks, designed to eliminate quite a few of the issues you may experience.

Lastly, we'll cover some tools and techniques designed to keep you safe.

For those interested in going deeper into security, you may wish to purchase *Joomla! WebSecurity* from Packt Publishing. It deals with the full gamut of security for your Joomla! site. It is available from `Amazon.com` and directly from `PacktPub.com`.

Setting permissions for your site

The following security tasks can eliminate a lot of common security issues very quickly. These represent some of the common issues you'll run into as a new Joomla! user.

Be sure and make a FULL BACKUP of the files, folders, and database before making any changes in this chapter.

How to do it...

Many times incorrect permissions can lead to a hacked site. In this example, the permissions are set for 777 - this is bad. Note these permissions have been intentionally set this way for this book, but it is a common mistake that new Joomla! users encounter.

Filename /	Filesize	Filetype	Last modified	Permissions
..				
administrator		File folder	6/18/2010 1:36:03 PM	0777
cache		File folder	6/24/2010 7:21:17 PM	0777
components		File folder	6/24/2010 3:55:05 PM	0777
images		File folder	6/24/2010 2:17:43 PM	0777
includes		File folder	6/18/2010 1:40:08 PM	0777
installation***		File folder	6/18/2010 1:40:32 PM	0777
language		File folder	6/18/2010 1:41:39 PM	0777
libraries		File folder	6/18/2010 1:41:59 PM	0777
logs		File folder	6/18/2010 1:43:12 PM	0777
media		File folder	6/24/2010 3:48:33 PM	0777
modules		File folder	6/24/2010 3:48:36 PM	0777
plugins		File folder	6/24/2010 3:55:03 PM	0777

There are very few legitimate reasons for a site to have permissions set to 777, which means ANYONE, can read or write to your site.

Setting permissions for directories

1. Open FileZilla and connect to your site.
2. "HIGHLIGHT" all your Directories.

3. Right click and select **Permissions**.

4. Type in **755** in the **Numeric value** field.

5. Check the box **Recurse into subdirectories**.

6. Select **Apply to directories only**.

7. Click **OK** to start the process.

 Make sure you select all the directories in the folder.

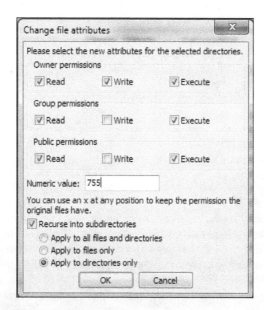

Once this process is complete, your directories and subdirectories will be set to the proper permission. Next, we'll repeat the process for files.

Setting permissions for files

1. Repeat the steps to highlight all files and folders in your Joomla! directory (usually `public_html`).

2. Right-click them - select **Permissions**.

3. In the **Numeric value** field, put **644**.

4. Click **Recurse into subdirectories**.

5. Click **Apply to files only**.

6. Click **OK**.

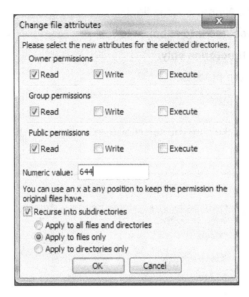

Your file and folder permissions are now set properly.

It didn't work!

Occasionally setting permissions as above won't have the affect you wish. This is likely due to the hosting configuration. If you get errors, return the permissions to what they were and contact your host. One thing you do not want is to have your files or folders require 777 to do anything.

Patching

Patching is a normal and regular part of running any software. Your website is made up of many software programs working in concert to create and display your online presence.

Patching actually means to update your software to the latest version. In this recipe, we'll look at how to patch your core Joomla! files and your extensions.

Joomla! core files

As Joomla! has regular updates, it's important to monitor and apply patches to the core Joomla! files.

1. Download the patches or full files from `joomla.org`. As an example, if you are running 1.5.17 there usually is a patch that will take you from 1.5.17 to say 1.5.18 (or whatever the latest is in the 1.5 series). You can download the entire version 1.5.xx (latest at the time you download it) and upload it to your site.

2. Make a full backup of your database and website and pull the copy off to another computer.

3. Unzip the files.

4. Connect with FileZilla FTP client to your website.

5. Copy all the files and overwrite your current files.

6. Test the site once the files are copied over.

 If you choose the entire 1.5.xx package to update your site, be sure you DO NOT copy over the Installation folder. Doing so will cause your production site to fail, until it is removed. Should you accidentally copy it - no worries - just remove it once done. Don't skip the step of full backup BEFORE you start. One word of caution - as Joomla! is open source, meaning the code is open and free to change to fit your needs, occasionally, a developer may make modifications to the core files. If your copy has been modified, then be sure you record and backup those changes. They will be lost when you copy the new files over them.

Patching extensions

Extensions are updated more frequently than the core Joomla! files and they can represent a large source of trouble. It is your job to keep up with the changes, not the developers. Even if they make a heroic effort to reach you, it's still your job.

▶   Obtain the patches from the developer. (I suggest the service www.salvusalerting. com to stay on top of the patch and vulnerability information.

▶   Make a full backup of your database and website and pull a copy off to another computer or a USB drive.

Review the particular extension's directions - but generally most extensions require removal of the old. You can try to do an install and *SOME* extensions will update right over the old version. You can review both methods below.

Method 1:

1. Make a full file and database backup.

2. Click **Extensions | Install / Uninstall**.

3. Install the extension.

4. Test site and extension.

5. Make another full file and database backup.

If the extension has been written to allow upgrading, then it will overwrite and not complain. If it complains, try method 2:

Method 2:

1. Make a full file and database backup.

2. Click **Extensions | Install /Uninstall**.

3. Uninstall the extension (component, module, plugin).

4. Upload and install the new extension.

5. Test site and extension.

6. Make another full file and database backup.

    Should you have modified forms, CSS, or graphics in a template, then be sure you add those changes back in if they were overwritten.

Using .htaccess and php.ini

Joomla! uses a special file called `htaccess.txt` that is standard issue on all Apache web servers. This file allows commands to be issued to instruct the webserver to take actions based on certain conditions.

The `htaccess.txt` file that is in every copy of Joomla!, has several specific instructions that offer some protection against specific types of hacks. Using this file helps avoid some common troubles that may visit your site.

How to do it...

Activating .htaccess protection

Please note before you start that the following steps might already be done.

1. Using your FileZilla FTP client - login into your site.

2. Locate the file called `htaccess.txt` in the root.

3. Right-click the file.

4. Choose **Rename**.

5. Rename it to `.htaccess` (don't forget the period before the name).

6. Test your site to make sure it's operating properly.

7. Close FileZilla.

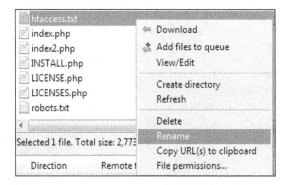

The preceding screenshot shows you how to follow these steps.

There's more...

The .htaccess file can provide you many other great tools. In this section, we'll take a look at a few of them such as blocking "evil" bots, blocking IPS, and adding a custom error page.

Don't worry about breaking anything, any changes you make to the .htaccess file can be easily reversed.

Blocking evil bots

Bots are helper applications that run in a variety of ways. There are, of course, good ones and bad ones. Examples of good ones are **Google crawler** or **Yahoo! crawler**. Examples of bad ones are **Zeus** and **BlackWidow**. In this recipe, we'll look at how to add protection to your .htaccess file to stop them.

How to do it...

We can add a bit of code to the .htaccess file to stop them.

1. Using FileZilla FTP client connect to your site.
2. Right -click on the .htaccess file.
3. *Ctrl+A* (in windows) and copy it.
4. Close the file.
5. Paste the copy into a notepad file - We do this so that we don't crash the site.

6. In the copy you just created, scroll to the bottom of the file and add the following: (This can be downloaded from the Packt website)

```
SetEnvIfNoCase User-Agent "^libwww-perl*" block_bad_bots
Deny from env=block_bad_bots
RewriteEngine On
RewriteCond %{HTTP_USER_AGENT} ^BlackWidow [OR]
RewriteCond %{HTTP_USER_AGENT} ^Bot\

RewriteCond %{HTTP_USER_AGENT} ^ChinaClaw [OR]
RewriteCond %{HTTP_USER_AGENT} ^Casper [OR]
RewriteCond %{HTTP_USER_AGENT} ^Custo [OR]
RewriteCond %{HTTP_USER_AGENT} ^DISCo [OR]
RewriteCond %{HTTP_USER_AGENT} ^Download\ Demon [OR]
RewriteCond %{HTTP_USER_AGENT} ^eCatch [OR]
RewriteCond %{HTTP_USER_AGENT} ^EirGrabber [OR]
RewriteCond %{HTTP_USER_AGENT} ^EmailSiphon [OR]
RewriteCond %{HTTP_USER_AGENT} ^EmailWolf [OR]
RewriteCond %{HTTP_USER_AGENT} ^Express\ WebPictures [OR]
RewriteCond %{HTTP_USER_AGENT} ^ExtractorPro [OR]
RewriteCond %{HTTP_USER_AGENT} ^EyeNetIE [OR]
RewriteCond %{HTTP_USER_AGENT} ^FlashGet [OR]
RewriteCond %{HTTP_USER_AGENT} ^GetRight [OR]
RewriteCond %{HTTP_USER_AGENT} ^GetWeb! [OR]
RewriteCond %{HTTP_USER_AGENT} ^Go!Zilla [OR]
RewriteCond %{HTTP_USER_AGENT} ^Go-Ahead-Got-It [OR]
RewriteCond %{HTTP_USER_AGENT} ^GrabNet [OR]
RewriteCond %{HTTP_USER_AGENT} ^Grafula [OR]
RewriteCond %{HTTP_USER_AGENT} ^HMView [OR]
RewriteCond %{HTTP_USER_AGENT} HTTrack [NC,OR]
RewriteCond %{HTTP_USER_AGENT} ^Image\ Stripper [OR]
RewriteCond %{HTTP_USER_AGENT} ^Image\ Sucker [OR]
RewriteCond %{HTTP_USER_AGENT} Indy\ Library [NC,OR]
RewriteCond %{HTTP_USER_AGENT} ^InterGET [OR]
RewriteCond %{HTTP_USER_AGENT} ^Internet\ Ninja [OR]
RewriteCond %{HTTP_USER_AGENT} ^JetCar [OR]
RewriteCond %{HTTP_USER_AGENT} ^JOC\ Web\ Spider [OR]
RewriteCond %{HTTP_USER_AGENT} ^larbin [OR]
RewriteCond %{HTTP_USER_AGENT} ^LeechFTP [OR]
RewriteCond %{HTTP_USER_AGENT} ^Mass\ Downloader [OR]
RewriteCond %{HTTP_USER_AGENT} ^MIDown\ tool [OR]
RewriteCond %{HTTP_USER_AGENT} ^Mister\ PiX [OR]
RewriteCond %{HTTP_USER_AGENT} ^Navroad [OR]
RewriteCond %{HTTP_USER_AGENT} ^NearSite [OR]
```

```
RewriteCond %{HTTP_USER_AGENT} ^NetAnts [OR]
RewriteCond %{HTTP_USER_AGENT} ^NetSpider [OR]
RewriteCond %{HTTP_USER_AGENT} ^Net\ Vampire [OR]
RewriteCond %{HTTP_USER_AGENT} ^NetZIP [OR]
RewriteCond %{HTTP_USER_AGENT} ^Octopus [OR]
RewriteCond %{HTTP_USER_AGENT} ^Offline\ Explorer [OR]
RewriteCond %{HTTP_USER_AGENT} ^Offline\ Navigator [OR]
RewriteCond %{HTTP_USER_AGENT} ^PageGrabber [OR]
RewriteCond %{HTTP_USER_AGENT} ^Papa\ Foto [OR]
RewriteCond %{HTTP_USER_AGENT} ^pavuk [OR]
RewriteCond %{HTTP_USER_AGENT} ^pcBrowser [OR]
RewriteCond %{HTTP_USER_AGENT} ^RealDownload [OR]
RewriteCond %{HTTP_USER_AGENT} ^ReGet [OR]
RewriteCond %{HTTP_USER_AGENT} ^SiteSnagger [OR]
RewriteCond %{HTTP_USER_AGENT} ^SmartDownload [OR]
RewriteCond %{HTTP_USER_AGENT} ^SuperBot [OR]
RewriteCond %{HTTP_USER_AGENT} ^SuperHTTP [OR]
RewriteCond %{HTTP_USER_AGENT} ^Surfbot [OR]
RewriteCond %{HTTP_USER_AGENT} ^tAkeOut [OR]
RewriteCond %{HTTP_USER_AGENT} ^Teleport\ Pro [OR]
RewriteCond %{HTTP_USER_AGENT} ^VoidEYE [OR]
RewriteCond %{HTTP_USER_AGENT} ^Web\ Image\ Collector [OR]
RewriteCond %{HTTP_USER_AGENT} ^Web\ Sucker [OR]
RewriteCond %{HTTP_USER_AGENT} ^WebAuto [OR]
RewriteCond %{HTTP_USER_AGENT} ^WebCopier [OR]
RewriteCond %{HTTP_USER_AGENT} ^WebFetch [OR]
RewriteCond %{HTTP_USER_AGENT} ^WebGo\ IS [OR]
RewriteCond %{HTTP_USER_AGENT} ^WebLeacher [OR]
RewriteCond %{HTTP_USER_AGENT} ^WebReaper [OR]
RewriteCond %{HTTP_USER_AGENT} ^WebSauger [OR]
RewriteCond %{HTTP_USER_AGENT} ^Website\ eXtractor [OR]
RewriteCond %{HTTP_USER_AGENT} ^Website\ Quester [OR]
RewriteCond %{HTTP_USER_AGENT} ^WebStripper [OR]
RewriteCond %{HTTP_USER_AGENT} ^WebWhacker [OR]
RewriteCond %{HTTP_USER_AGENT} ^WebZIP [OR]
RewriteCond %{HTTP_USER_AGENT} ^Wget [OR]
RewriteCond %{HTTP_USER_AGENT} ^Widow [OR]
RewriteCond %{HTTP_USER_AGENT} ^WWWOFFLE [OR]
RewriteCond %{HTTP_USER_AGENT} ^Xaldon\ WebSpider [OR]
RewriteCond %{HTTP_USER_AGENT} ^Zeus
RewriteRule ^.* - [F,L]
```

How it works...

The Apache server looks at a part of the visitor's data that comes with their request and reviews it to see if it's a bot. If it is, it then looks at the User Agent String. This is a name that helps to identify this agent. It compares it to the preceding list and if a match is found, then the connection is in essence refused. While not foolproof, it can stop many of the bad bots out there.

A User Agent String looks like:

Googlebot/2.1 (**+**`http://www.google.com/bot.html`)

If we told the `.htaccess` file to drop (or block) Googlebot, then Google would never index or crawl our site.

In our `.htaccess`, we have told it to drop the bad bots only. A word of caution - bad - bots are invented all the time - thus you'll need to stay on top of them. The subject of `.htaccess` is a complex one.

Remember a large part of site attacks are conducted and are successful because the site admin did not take the precautions and gave away information.

Most of these precautions work through the `.htaccess` file which is read every time the site is accessed.

Preventing unauthorized directory browsing

You might have noticed in the sub-directories of a Joomla! site that there is an `index.html` file that contains this:

```
<html><body bgcolor="#FFFFFF"></body></html>
```

This is strictly to prevent someone from 'browsing' your subdirectories and seeing the content.

If that `index.html` file gets erased or changed; the contents of your subdirectory will lay bare.

Adding a single line to your `.htaccess` file will prevent directory listing - adding a secondary layer of protection.

Following the previous instructions in earlier recipes for opening the `.htaccess` and making a safe copy you will want to add this line at the bottom of the `.htaccess`:

> ▶ `options All -Indexes`

After adding this, you'll need to reupload your `.htaccess`.

Adding a universal error page

Hackers often trigger errors on sites to learn more about the operating system, version levels, locations of files, and more. Providing a universal error page will keep the bad guys from learning what errors are triggered by what action. As an added benefit you will be providing a higher level of customer service.

Following the previous instructions in earlier recipes for opening the `.htaccess` and making a safe copy you will want to add these lines at the bottom of the `.htaccess`:

```
RewriteCond %{REQUEST_FILENAME} !-f
RewriteCond %{REQUEST_FILENAME} !-d
RewriteRule ^.*$ /dir/error.php [L]
```

 Please note, the `/dir/error.php` points to a directory of your choosing that contains a script that will produce the error page you want.

Disabling the server "Banner"

Again a lot of security is handled around NOT giving the bad guys information. Turning off the server signature or "banner" is vital. It's a quick process and can be done at the Apache server level or something as simple as adding this line to your `.htaccess` file:

```
serverSignature Off
```

Using php.ini to protect your site

The php.ini file stores directives that enable you to configure and change your PHP setup. You can change the execution time of a PHP script and give it more or less time. You can allocate more memory, you can change certain global variables. For a complete list of the directives please see this URL: http://php.net/manual/en/ini.core.php.

Settings to protect you in php.ini

`php.ini` is a special file that instructs the PHP server on how to perform certain tasks or to restrict the server, configure its operation, and so on. Your site may not have this file in place, or your host may have to change it.

As a precaution, you can add these to a local `php.ini` file, but if you notice 'odd' behavior after you do, then contact your host to have these settings added.

1. Using FileZilla FTP client login to your site.

2. Locate the file in the root called `php.ini` - note it may not exist.

   ❑ If it does not exist, then use notepad or other text editor to create it. Give it the permissions 644.

3. Right-click to edit the file.

4. If these are not in the file, then add them to the `php.ini` file.

```
register_globals = off (or = 0) (this function GONE in php 5.3.0
and later so no worries.)
allow_url_fopen = 0
allow_url_include = 0
define('RG_EMULATION', 0)
expose_php =off   (this suppresses error messages)
magic_quotes_gpc = off (or =0)
magic_quotes_runtime = off (or =0)
```

> It's worth noting that as in PHP the language matures, some of these settings are being added to PHP itself, preventing you from having to do this. However, there are a lot of PHP 4.xx servers out there still. As an example, `register_globals` is disabled by default starting at PHP 4.2.0 and is gone in 5.3.0, however, it's included here to be sure you can turn it off if it is on. Having it set in your site configuration from 5.3.x on should not impact you. This setting is one that is quickly going away.

How it works...

Security is not something you can buy and install. While there are commercial products available, security is a layered approach. In other words, you want to put up multiple layers of defence against attackers. These steps, while simple, eliminate quite a bit of trouble you may encounter.

The `.htaccess` is a directory-level access file that issues commands specific to that directory. As you can see we place our `.htaccess` into the root of our website, instructing Apache to apply the rules to the root directory and files down. So it applies globally to your site.

We could use `.htaccess` to turn on SSL, build specific error page redirects or even use it to protect a specific directory. It is a very powerful tool in your arsenal.

`php.ini` is a file that allows you to modify the settings of PHP's run-time environment. It does require your host to have installed (most do by default) suPHP. In our example, we adjusted some settings to help protect our site.

We can additionally add other settings such as these:

```
php_flag upload_max_filesize 10M
php_value max_execution_time 30
```

These commands instruct PHP to limit our upload size for files to 10 megabytes, and restrict a script to 30 seconds. This prevents a poorly written PHP script from running away. These are only examples and may or may not apply to your site.

For more information about `php.ini` and `.htaccess`, please refer to the Packt Publishing book *Joomla! Web Security*.

Denying specific IP addresses

As you probably know, if a computer is attached to a network, such as the Internet, it is assigned an IP or Internet Protocol address. This IP address uniquely identifies the computer, where it lives in the world, and much more.

When a person comes to your site, the Apache web server (and other software like firewalls) will record that information and use it to return the requested information.

We would like it if all visitors to our sites had our best interest in mind, but sadly it's not true. Occasionally, a person visiting may try to break in, or a comprised desktop is taken over by hackers and used to attack.

Other cases may include the need to block a country or network address range.

In this recipe, we'll look at how to block or deny an IP address.

Getting ready

As this is an example only, use `10.100.100.1` as your example.

How to do it...

Denying specific IP address(es)

Occasionally, you will need to block an IP that is attempting to or has broken into your site. The BEST solution is to ask the HOST to block it at the firewall. However, sometimes that's not feasible. In that event we can include them in the .htaccess file.

1. Using FileZilla FTP client connect to your site.
2. Right-click on the `.htaccess` file.
3. *Ctrl+A* (in Windows) and copy it.
4. Close the file.
5. Paste the copy into a notepad file. It is important to note that an incorrect setting in `.htaccess` can cause 500 server errors. This is not a permanent condition and reversing the changes will fix this. By working in a text editor, we can quickly restore the changes. Additional benefits to the use of a text editor are the ability to work offline and only upload the changes once you have completed them.

6. In the copy you just created, scroll to the bottom of the file and add the following:

```
order allow,deny
deny from 10.100.100.1
allow from all
```

 The 10.100.100.1 represents the IP address in question. You can repeat the deny from <ip address> as often as you need. One point if you have a large amount of entries in this, you will risk slowing down your site.

7. Save the text file as `htaccess-new.txt`.
8. Returning again to the FTP - RENAME the .htaccess to `htaccess-original`.txt.
9. Upload the `htaccess.txt` file.
10. Rename `htaccess-net.txt` file to `.htaccess`.

Your site will no longer allow visitors from those IP's to visit.

How it works...

The web server can maintain a list of addresses to block. If an IP address that is unwanted and is in the list attempts to visit, then the connection will be refused. You could even redirect them to another site if you wanted.

It is important to note, that with the nature of dynamic IP addresses, this may be a short-lived solution if a dedicated attacker is attempting to break in.

Summary

In this chapter, we scratched the surface on security issues. These recipes are intended to get you started and you are encouraged to learn more about site security.

In this chapter, you were introduced to the very powerful `.htaccess` file and some of its many uses. The examples included in this bloc-specific IP's and Bots, protecting directories and, as no one likes to see a 404 page, custom error pages.As Joomla! runs natively on PHP, the `php.ini` file will likely be something you'll configure at some point in your site's life.

Learning a bit more about these tools will pay off in no time for you.

11
Joomla! 1.6

In this chapter, we will cover:

- ► Joomla! 1.6 **Access Control List (ACL)**
- ► Access levels for front-end viewing
- ► Users and Groups in 1.6
- ► Access control by article
- ► Working with the new Category Manager
- ► Extension Manager

Introduction

As this chapter is being written Joomla! 1.6 is in beta 7, thus this information is subject to change.

In this chapter, we'll look at a few recipes that cover the portions of Joomla! 1.6 that are brand new.

The 1.6 version has several exciting features such as unlimited nesting of categories - or in other words, categories, which can hold categories, which can, in turn, hold categories. Each can be tuned to the specific site's need. **Access Control List (ACL)** which is native to Joomla! 1.6 and much more.

We cover this and a few other new gems that are found in 1.6.

Joomla! 1.6 ACL

One of the most powerful additions to the new version of Joomla! is the Access Control List system or ACL. The ACL is broken down into three key areas as follows:

- ▸ **Global Configuration**: It controls ACL system wide. Permissions flow from here to other ACL systems.

- ▸ **Category ACL**: This controls the Categories in Joomla! 1.6. It receives its top permissions from the Global Configuration. Permissions flow down within the categories to lower categories.

- ▸ **Article ACL**: This receives inherited permission from the Category ACL. It only affects the individual articles it is used on.

> You can easily lock out super user access to your site if you incorrectly set permissions in the Global Configuration ACL.
>
> The information in this chapter is subject to change, as the ACL covered in this book is Joomla! 1.6 beta 7.
>
> It may change before it goes into production.

It is very important that if you intend to make any changes to the ACL you understand the effects it will have. If you do not have a good grasp of the ACL, I strongly suggest you simply take the default settings of the ACL system and leave it at that. Take the time to learn the ACL system before making changes.

If you do decide to change the ACL, make sure you have a backup of your DATABASE first. That way you can quickly restore and unlock yourself.

There is another means to unlock an administrator account and we'll cover that shortly.

Some terms that will help you understand how this all ties together:

- ▸ **Users**: This is a person who is either visiting or logging into your site.
- ▸ **Groups**: This group, or groups the person can belong too.
- ▸ **Access Level**: These are rights (*deny, allow*) that are assigned to various functions (*create, login, admin...*) to the groups.

In essence, a user (person) is given an account, which is assigned to a group. That group is granted or denied permissions to do specific tasks.

Permissions flow from the top-most level down

Here is a graphic showing Default Groups installed using Sample Data from Joomla! 1.6, Beta 7:

In this case, the top-most group is **Registered** users. Thus users in the lower groups who belong to the subgroups of **Author**, **Editor**, or **Publisher** can inherit the permissions of **Registered.**

It is worth noting that **Author** represents the parent group of **Editor** and **Publisher**. **Editor** represents the parent group of **Publisher**. However, **Shop Suppliers** is a child of **Author** and a peer to the **Editor** group.

A change within **Publisher** will not affect **Shop Suppliers**. But a change in **Editor** will affect **Publisher** and **Shop Suppliers**.

Changing any permission in **Registered** users will change all these groups. Here's a quick example:

Super Administrators and administrators by default are allowed to log into the Administrator Console.

If we change **Registered** users permissions (by default) from (**...**) to **Allow** in these two fields, then everyone in any group below **Registered** users will be allowed to login as **Super Admin**:

In this recipe, we'll be reviewing how to change the **GLOBAL ACL**. -- Move with caution - permissions up ahead.

Getting ready

Before you start, revisit the recipe on backing up your MySQL database. Make a complete backup in the event you lock yourself out.

Here is a view of the default ACL list as it comes installed by Joomla!

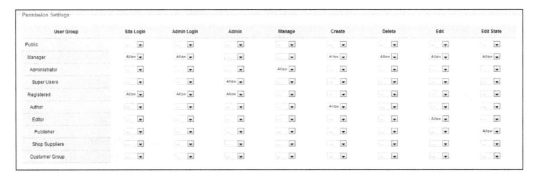

Permission Settings

User Group	Site Login	Admin Login	Admin	Manage	Create	Delete	Edit	Edit State
Public	...	...	...	...	...	...	...	...
Manager	Allow	Allow	...	...	Allow	Allow	Allow	Allow
Administrator	...	...	...	Allow	...	...	...	...
Super Users	...	...	Allow	...	...	...	...	...
Registered	Allow	Allow	Allow	...	...	...	...	...
Author	...	...	...	...	Allow	...	...	...
Editor	...	...	...	...	...	...	Allow	...
Publisher	...	...	...	...	...	...	...	Allow
Shop Suppliers	...	...	...	...	...	...	...	...
Customer Group	...	...	...	...	...	...	...	...

While this is difficult to read, what you have is the following basic rules to follow:

- ▶ (**...**) Is default - it inherits the group above it. In the event of **Public**, it is a *deny by default*.
- ▶ (**Allow**) is an explicit command to allow the group and all other groups under it the rights to take an action - such as edit, delete, or even become the Super Administrator.
- ▶ (**Deny**) is an explicit command to deny the group and all other groups under it the rights to take an action. Again - edit, create, delete, and even login as Super Administrator.

Rules flow down from Public to Super Administrator. One scenario is if you feel you should deny the Public right to login as Admin. Putting **Deny** in the admin field for the **Public** group will lock out the Super Administrator.

It is better in the Global ACL to leave the **Public** group as (**...**) which is a deny for any users in the **Public** group.

How to do it...

1. Log in to the Joomla! Administrator.
2. Click **Global Configuration**.
3. Choose a group to change the permissions for. In this case, we'll be using the sample data.

4. Changing the following settings for the group **Customer Group** would give any users in the Customer Group the rights to login as the Super Administrator:

This would not allow me to login on the front of the site, but would allow me as an admin to login. All permissions work this way - so be careful.

How it works...

As we touched on the permissions in the **Global Configuration** control everything top down. Further, the current design (Beta 7) has many opportunities to lock you out, or to let the wrong people in.

Here's a great way to look at how permissions flow:

Global Configuration | Category Manager | Articles <stop>

By changing permission in Global Configuration, you change the permissions by **Group**. Within those groups, you have users, and they will inherit the permissions.

Categories inherit permissions and pass them down to the categories below them. Lastly, articles have the ability to restrict who can do what per article.

There's more...

The ACL in Joomla! 1.6, will take you some time to understand its complexities. In this next recipe, we'll peer deeper into the ACL and look at the group level access.

Group level access

While the group level itself cannot be altered directly, outside of the ACL, you can change some of the ways it gets its information.

1. Login to the Joomla! Administrator.

2. Select **Users | Groups**.

3. You will see something similar to this:

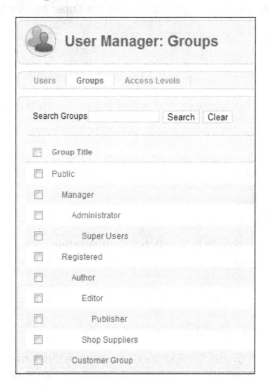

In this example, the **Group**, **Customer Group** will inherit ALL permissions from Registered Users Group. In this example, changing permissions in the Registered Users Group will cause the permission to flow down to the Customer Group.

Let's say you wish to make **Customer Group** a subgroup of **Public** instead – and, thus, not worrying about permissions from **Registered** flowing down. To change its parent group, follow these steps:

4. Click **Customer Group**.

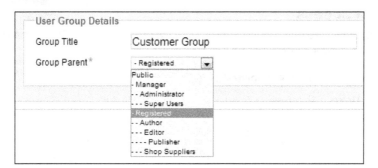

5.   It is a member of **Registered**. To change its membership, click **Public**.

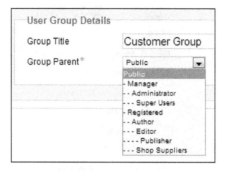

This has now moved the group **Customer Group** to **Public**. And thus, all users belonging to **Customer Group**, will immediately take on the rights of Public and lose the other rights. Moving to public, will by default give them the least amount of rights.

Users and Groups

Users can belong to more than one group, which can make for a challenge. If you have a registered user and accidentally insert them into a group that has Super User Access, they will then get Super User Access. Let's review how to change a user's group.

1.   Login to administrator.

2.   Open **Users | Groups**.

3.   Select your user you wish to change the group level of.

4.   The following is an example of a **Registered** User Group

This is where it can get tricky. This user currently only belongs to the **Registered** users group, which by default is given Public access as well.

If I 'added' them to the **Publisher** group - the result would be as follows:

Notice, they inherited the permissions of the **Editor** and **Author**. That makes sense as **Publisher** is a higher order user, and thus would have those permissions.

In the event you meant to select **Customer Group** instead, you would uncheck the **Publisher** Group and check the **Customer Group**. That would result in this:

See the problem? You had previously had **Publisher**, which brought with it the permissions of **Author** and **Editor** as well. Simply unchecking **Publisher** and checking **Customer Group**, left those permissions intact. You may not have wanted that.

To be fair, this is being written around BETA 7 and may change before production. However, be aware of it in the event it does not.

Unselecting all the permissions auto checked, would then leave me with what I wanted in the first place:

If you are ever in doubt, review the **User Manager** again - and you'll see a column like this one that indicates the groups a user belongs too.

Access levels

Another portion of the overall ACL is the custom access level which allows you to control who sees what resources on the front end of your website. Think of this as read permissions for the public portion of your site.

Unlike the ACL though, Access Levels do not inherit permissions. They are set by article. Say that an article is set for authors only. Then, only the authors group can view that from the front end. A Super Administrator, who logs into the front end, will not see the article. Logging in the back end of Joomla! as an administrator allows the Super Administrator to see and edit the article.

Setting the Access Level:

1. Log in into the Joomla! Administrator Console.
2. Click **Users | Access Levels**.
3. Click **New** to create a new Access Level (or choose one).
4. In our example we see the following:

In this example, the **BookUser** Access Level is assigned to the **Author** groups. If the user is not a member of the **Author** group when they log in on the front they will be able to see the content assigned.

Next when an article is created, you can assign the Access Level for it. Here is our example article that will be viewed by **Author** group members only.

We set the level in the field called **Access** as shown in the preceding screenshot.

 Wait! It doesn't say **Author**, it says **Registered**. That's correct! Remember that **Author** is a child of the **Registered** group. We assign access to **Registered**, for the **Author** group.

I strongly suggest you set up a demo site to play with and learn the ACL very well. Or simply leave everything default and avoid changing these fields and it will work just fine as well.

Help! I've locked myself out of my 1.6 site!

Given the complexity of the ACL, it is a simple matter to change up the permissions to the point that you could lock out your Super Administrator account. That's a bad thing to do.

The other way in, is through a "back door" that allows you to log in to your website. To do this you need to be able to access your files via FTP and you will need to know your Super Administrator name.

One thing to remember in Joomla! 1.6, is the default 'admin' doesn't have to be called admin anymore.

To use this back door locate your configuration.php file and open it for editing via FTP.

Add this line of code to the bottom of configuration.php:

```
public $root_user="MyAdmin";
```

replacing MyAdmin with the name of your Super Administrator account.

Save and close the FTP client.

You should be able to return to the administrator login and log in as normal.

Once you do - go back and fix the ACL, and remove the line you added from your configuration.php file.

Working with new category manager

In Joomla!, articles are segmented by sections and categories. In Joomla! 1.5, you had the ability to lay out your site via this section and category segmentation.

In Joomla! 1.6, the sections are gone in favor of multiple nested categories setup. In other words, it can look something like this:

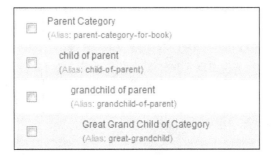

This enables administrators to set up unlimited levels of nested categories. You can control access to each of the various levels using the new ACL system in Joomla! 1.6.

Getting ready

There is very little work to do in preparation for this, except to figure out what your categories are. Don't worry if you aren't sure of the all the categories-you'll just need to have to think about a few categories as shown in the preceding screenshot:

How to do it...

1. Login into the Joomla! Administrator using your administrator username and password.

2. Open **Content | Category Manager**.

Once opened, you'll see the following screen:

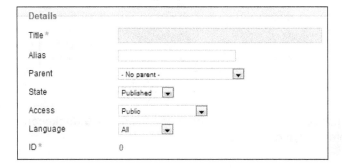

3. The following steps are used to create the category:

  ▶ **Title**: Fill in the title of the category.

  ▶ **Alias**: This field, alias, is automatically filled in based on the title and is used for the Search Engine Optimized URL.

  ▶ **Parent**: This is the parent (if any) of the category. If this is a subcategory you would select its parent. You can make these as deep as you need.

  ▶ **State**: **Published** or **Unpublished**.

  ▶ **Access**: This is the access level (acl) that is allowed to view it. In this example, it is viewable by **Public**.

  ▶ Click **Save** or **Save and Close**.

  Let's go through a real scenario. In this example, we'll create a main category that will hold our book articles.

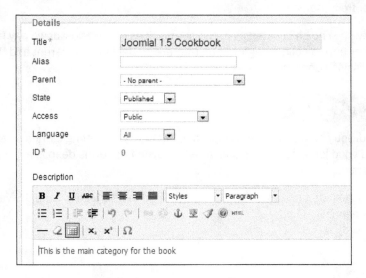

After we save this we'll want to add chapters under as follows

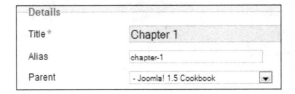

As you can see the **Parent** category is the **Joomla! 1.5 Cookbook**. After we fill out a few more categories they resemble this:

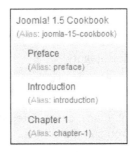

Each of the subcategories is the child of the main Joomla! 1.5 Cookbook category.

How it works...

Each of the subcategories can be a parent and a child. Each child category inherits permissions from its parent. But each child can change or alter their own permissions such that they differ from the parent.

As long as they have no child categories, the permissions will not flow down any further. However - if they have a child category, then they are by definition, a parent and the same rules for permissions apply here as well.

There's more...

As you learned, you can place several levels deep categories. Getting carried away is probably not a good idea, but having two, three, or even four levels deep is a great way to segment content.

The following screenshot shows an Article being paired to a Category. Note the various levels of different categories:

The main category in this sample data example from Joomla! 1.6, is **Sample Data-Articles**. The rest fall as sub, *sub-sub*, *sub-sub-sub* or even four levels deep in the case of the templates articles.

Now that you have a good idea on how to establish the categories, and various levels, the next recipe will show you how to use the new access rules of the category manager.

Access rules of category manager

Each category and subcategory in Joomla! 1.6 can be set individually to control each user group. This gives you a very fine-grained control over the articles and categories on your site.

If, for instance, you wish the group *manager* to have ability to create content, but not delete it, for say a *Pricing category*, then you simply set their ability to delete to **Deny**.

However, there is a dark side to this, and that is that, permissions flow down to subcategories. If you set in the very top category Deny on any field, it flows down to all user groups in every category. This will require you to pay attention, so you do not lock yourself out or open yourself up to the world.

How does this work?

The following is the default (as of Beta 7) ACL states for a newly created category:

This states the following by group:

- ▶ **Public** may not **Create**, **Delete**, **Edit**, or **Edit State**

- ▶ **Manager**, **Administrator**, and **Super Users** can **Create**, **Delete**, **Edit**, and **Edit State**

- ▶ **Registered** users, like **Public** are restricted to viewing only

- ▶ **Author** users are allowed **Create** rights but nothing else

- ▶ **Editor** users may create and edit only

- ▶ **Publisher** users may **Create**, **Edit**, and **Edit State**

- ▶ **Shop Suppliers** and **Customer Group** are allowed create rights only

Please note this applies to this category only.

Using our previous recipe scenario, let's say the Joomla! 1.5 cookbook categories would only have Create, Delete, Edit rights only for the Author. The administrative users would retain full rights and the Shop Suppliers and Customer Group would not have any rights. Then, in that case, the ACL for the main chapter would look like this:

	Create	Delete	Edit	Edit State
Public	⊖	⊖	⊖	⊖
Manager	✔	✔	✔	✔
Administrator	✔	✔	✔	✔
Super Users	✔	✔	✔	✔
Registered	⊖	⊖	⊖	⊖
Author	✔	✔	✔	⊖
Editor	✔	✔	✔	⊖
Publisher	✔	✔	✔	✔
Shop Suppliers	⊖	⊖	⊖	⊖
Customer Group	⊖	⊖	⊖	⊖

Take a look at the subtle difference between the two.

Here is where it gets important to think through ACLs. Remember in our example, we have this structure:

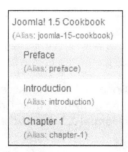

You see the default Parent category is **Joomla! 1.5 CookBook** and the ACL setting for **Public** for that category is as follows:

	Create	Delete	Edit	Edit State
Public	⊖	⊖	⊖	⊖

If I click the **Create** tab, I see the following:

You see in the **Create** tab, it says **Inherit**. That means, whatever the category above it gets, each subcategory gets the same.

If you change the Create in the Joomla! CookBook main category to allow then it and all the subcategories will look like this:

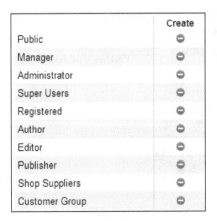

The main ACL and the subcategories, or nested categories, each get **Create** in the **Public** group. This means that anyone in that group can create something in that category.

I am sure you didn't mean to give anyone in the world, access to your site to create content. Thus, you will likely want to go back and Deny the Public Group rights to create. Let's set the public to Deny in our main category, **Joomla! 1.5 Cookbook**.

See what happens?

	Create
Public	⊖
Manager	⊖
Administrator	⊖
Super Users	⊖
Registered	⊖
Author	⊖
Editor	⊖
Publisher	⊖
Shop Suppliers	⊖
Customer Group	⊖

As you can see the effect of setting the **Public** group to deny caused the same permission to flow down to all groups for this category and subcategories. In effect, we locked everyone out of the ability to create content for this group.

What we should have done is set the **Public** field to **Inherit** as follows:

	Create
Public	⊖
Manager	✔
Administrator	✔
Super Users	✔
Registered	⊖
Author	✔
Editor	✔
Publisher	✔
Shop Suppliers	✔
Customer Group	✔

As you can see, just setting the **Public** to **Inherit** rather than **Deny**, put the permissions to their previous and proper levels.

In summary, permissions flow down. If you have two subcategories that belong to the same parent, then permissions only flow from parent to child category. This means you can change one child category's permission without impacting the other.

If, however, you have a child of a child, then any changes made to the Parent Category will be propagated throughout the entire chain, affecting all the permissions below it.

Best practices with working with the Category ACL

In order to keep things working and not introduce problems that could take hours to find, always consider carefully before making a change to a Parent category. This can be a subcategory as well as the top-level category. In a nutshell, permission flows down from where they are to the next levels below it. But they do not move sideways.

Extensions

This recipe, will not be covering any API or coding development of extensions, but rather will discuss the management of them. In 1.6, a lot of work has gone into improving their interaction.

In this set of recipes, you'll see some tips and tricks - this section will be a quick - catch all about extensions.

Let's start with a new look at all the new features in the Module Manager.

How to do it...

Installation of a module, extension, or plugin hasn't changed all that much. There are a lot of changes in the management of modules. Let's manage a module to see the changes.

Setting publishing start and stop time of module:

1. Login to the Joomla! Administrator Console.
2. Select **Extensions | Module Manager**.
3. Select the Module you wish to manage.
4. Find **Publish Start** and **Publish Stop**.
5. Fill in the dates and times.

Here you see like the articles in Joomla! 1.5, the ability for a module to turn on and turn off at specified times.

6. Optionally, leave a note in the module.
7. Find the **Note** field, fill it out, click **Save**.

In this case, a note was added that we can see from the Module Manager screen. This is a view from Module Manager.

Setting the access level for modules:

While still in the Module Manager and having selected the module of your choice, find the Access Level drop-down:

You can select the Access level of the viewer. A simple example may be someone who has specific modules they are allowed to have for their account. This will enable them to see just that, while others without that access will not be able to log in to see it.

How it works...

Module management has taken a great leap forward in 1.6. Now a module can be treated with nearly the same control an article can.

The system has been expanded to include the ability to start and stop publishing, the ability to specify who can see the module and as we'll see a terrific level of control of where it can be displayed.

There's more...

The Module Manager has an enhanced menu display system.

The above example shows all our menus in this website and the module assignment.

We can set a single menu or many, all, or none.

To set a module to show on all menus

1. Open the module.
2. Pull down the **Module Assignment** drop-down list.
3. Select **On All Pages**.
4. Save.

To set a module to show on no pages

1. Open the module.
2. Pull down the **Module Assignment** drop-down list.
3. Select **No Pages**.
4. Save.

To set a module to show on selected pages

1. Open the module.
2. Pull down the **Module Assignment** drop-down list.
3. Select **Only on the pages selected**.
4. Click in the checkboxes the pages you want to include.
5. Save.
6. This module will only be shown on the pages selected.

To set a module to show on all pages, except those selected

1. Open the module.
2. Pull down the **Module Assignment** drop-down list.
3. Select **On all pages except those selected**.
4. Choose the pages you want to exclude.
5. Save.
6. This module will not be shown on the pages selected.

Other new extension manager features

As the preceding screenshot indicates, there are some new features you may not be aware of in 1.6.

Update:

This is used to update your Joomla! extensions. If an extension is available, you'll be able to update it from here.

Discover:

Occasionally, you might run into an extension that is too large to upload through the traditional means. You can upload the extension to the server and click **Discover**. This will find and install the extension for you.

Warnings:

This handy tool will review your server setup and tell you if any settings are incorrect, or could be better optimized for Joomla!. It is a good idea, to use this right after you install the base Joomla! 1.6. That way you discover errors before you start building the site.

Extension permissions

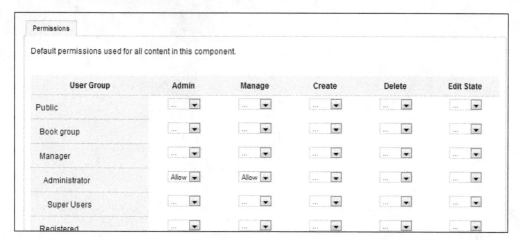

The Extension Manager (and Module Manager) both offer a light switch ICON that houses the ACL for them. As you can see the familiar ACL allows us to change the permissions for modules and Extension Manager.

Don't touch

There are not likely many scenarios where you will need to change this. If you do, be sure and have a backup. It is wise to leave this to advanced users of Joomla! 1.6

Appendix

Usernames, passwords and database reference sheet

This will allow you to capture all your usernames, server name, and other information in one place. REMEMBER to keep this record in a very safe place.

FTP Information: _____

FTP Server or IP Address: _____

FTP User: _____

FTP Password: _____

FTP Port (Optional): _____ **(typically Port: 21)**

FTP Root Path (FTP layer only): _____

Joomla! Administrator Information:

Site Domain: _____

Site Name: _____

Admin Password: _____

Admin Email: _____

Database Server Information:

DBType: (default is MySQL) _____

Host Name: _____

User Name: _____

Database Name: _____

Hosting information:

Login Name: _____

Login Password: _____

IP Address: _____

Tech Support Phone: _____

Tech Support email: _____

Other: _____

Other: _____

cPanel® information:

Login URL for cPanel®: _____

Username for cPanel®: _____

Password for cPanel®: _____

Turning the legacy mode on or off

When Joomla! 1.5.x was released, the former and original Joomla! 1.0.x came to be known as Legacy. 1.5. It can run and support 1.0.x extensions and templates. There are cases such as migrations, custom-built extensions, and others that may cause the need for this. If possible, do not turn on the Legacy mode. Try to search for either the updated 1.5 version or an equivalent version. I suspect there are many sites still running 1.0.x and at some point they will migrate to Joomla! 1.5.x. and as such, learning about legacy mode will be important for moving to 1.5.

In order for Joomla 1.5.x to support and run older components, modules, and mambots from the 1.0 family, there's a special layer called Legacy mode.

This quick recipe will show you how to activate and deactivate Legacy mode.

How to do it...

1. Log in to the Administrator Console.

2. Click **Extensions | Plugin Manager**.

3. Once in **Plugin Manager**, locate the plugin called **System Legacy**.

4. To enable Legacy mode, click the red X (assume it's off).

5. To disable Legacy mode, click the green check.

How it works...

Legacy mode is a Plugin that emulates Joomla! 1.0. The difference between 1.0 and 1.5 extensions is great, and with this, developers and users can continue to use their 1.0 extensions. While using this you might experience some degraded performance and the site may be more vulnerable to attack, based on the extensions you are using.

Changing the favorite icon

In some browsers, your site can display an "ICON" in the address bar. The default Joomla! site shows the Joomla! icon.

This is easy and quick to change. It gives your site a nice custom look and removes the Joomla! logo at the same time.

Getting ready

You'll need a graphic of size 100 x 100 pixels, typically .png format. Additionally, you can use a 32 x 32 or 16 x 16 graphic.

The Open-source graphics tool GIMP or commercial tools like Photoshop or Snagit are some of the graphics applications available for your use.

You will require a FTP client and any browser.

How to do it...

1. Visit - `http://www.favicongenerator.com/`.

2. Upload your 100 x 100 pixel graphic.

3. Click **Generate a file** with the extension `.ico`.

4. Save it to your local disk.

5. Rename the file to `favicon.ico`.

6. Connect to your website using your FTP client.

7. Upload the `<file>.ico`. `/joomla/templates/<your template>` directory.

How it works...

The `favicon` is loaded up by the browser each time a page is called from your template directory. You can see this by opening the site and looking in the address bar.

Setting up a site in a subfolder

Occasionally, you will want a subfolder for a site - such as `http://developmentsite.example.com`.

While not always preferable, for security reasons – it's very simple to do.

Getting ready

We require the following:

1. Fresh copy of Joomla! 1.5.21 or greater.

2. Setting up a new database.

3. Make sure your host helps you set up a subdomain in your DNS.

How to do it...

1. Connect to your web server with your FTP client (FileZilla).

2. Navigate to the root directory of your subdomain.

3. Upload a fresh copy of Joomla! into it - be careful you don't overwrite your current site.

4. Open your database manager (typically phpMyAdmin) and create a database - record the username and password.

5. Open your browser and navigate to the new subfolder:

    ```
    http://www.example.com/subdomain
    ```

The normal Joomla! install should commence now.

How it works...

The browser treats this folder like any other folder. The browser will load the `index.php` file and run it.

You can load up any extension, template, module, or anything else.

This is a great way to have a development site reside on your production server. The positives to this are you will know if you have any server-related issues. It also makes it simple and quick to move from development to production.

The downside is if you have a script run-away with itself, it could impact your production site.

The best practice is to put the development site on another server or a local machine.

There's more...

Depending on your host's configuration, you can set up a true subdomain, rather than a subfolder. The steps to do that are beyond the scope of this book. Please contact your host for assistance on this.

Questions to ask a prospective host

This recipe is slightly off-topic from "doing stuff"- it's targeted rather at education. There are, many hosts out there and not all are good. While I don't believe that any host tries to be bad, I think that it boils down to some hosts simply are better.

This quick recipe has few questions you should ask your host.

How to do it...

Call them up or contact them on their site and ask these questions.

Q: Do you allow me to archive and review my log files?

A: Host should allow you to do this - they may offer you a couple of methods to do this, but overall they should say Yes.

Q: Do you own and manage your server equipment? Or do you sublease equipments from a big collocation. [This happens more times than you know]

A: They will most likely not tell you, they will likely state they are the host. One means to find out is to ask for a few sample sites they are hosting, and do a 'tracert' to the IP address of the samples. This will many times resolve to the true destination. Other options include hosting resellers. These are, often, a great option if they are backed up by a great host. Take time to explore and find out what works best for your business.

Q: In the event of a power outage, how long can your data center run?

A: They will offer varying degrees of answers on this - but the simple answer is they have generators and fuel 'contracts' and will not shut be down during a power outage.

Q: Can I adjust and change my `htaccess` and my `php.ini` file?

A: The answer you want is yes. Many hosts will allow this but some do not.

Q: What Server Operating System do you run?

A: Make sure it's some form of Linux. Examples include: **CentOs**, **Denbian**, **Ubuntu**, **RedHat**, **Fedora**, and others.

Q: Can I use SSH or SecureFTP?

A: The answer should be yes - if not move on.

Q: If I am hacked, what is the procedure?

A: Many hosts will simply shut you down and not help you - while this is done to protect the integrity of their network and other clients, it's unhelpful if you are attacked. Note - having a really good backup plan will mitigate this. At the end of the day, site security is your responsibility. Doing everything you can to protect your site will prevent most problems.

Q: What is your internal procedure to update your servers? Am I responsible for updating my own server and applications?

A: This answer will depend on the plan you select. Unless you are selecting a box you manage, they should tell you they do it - but spot check from time to time. This is typically rare and happens with small and understaffed hosting companies.

Q: What administrative panel do you offer me?

A: Some popular ones are cPanel® and Plesx. You might even hear WHM which is offered typically, but not always, in a reseller option.

Q: In your building — Does the portion of your data center that houses the servers have windows to the outside?

A: The correct answer should be no.

Q: Do you do a criminal background check on your employees?

A: This is state dependant, but good to know – check with your attorney for State or Country legal rules.

Q: What type of backup and recovery options do you provide me?

A: They may offer you a lot of different answers. They may offer a paid service or a CRON (timer-based) job that helps for backup. They may not offer anything at all. At the end of the day it's your content and you are ultimately responsible for backups.

Q: If you do a restore for me, how long can I expect it to take and what costs are associated with it?

A: Many hosts state 72 hours to restore a site and sometimes a fee.

How it works...

There are many hosts to choose from and taking the time to find out the particulars of your choice before buying can save you a lot of headache later on.

Checking and updating your server software

This is an advanced task and should be performed by more experienced users. This is only done on a dedicated machine or an unmanaged VPS. This will not apply to shared hosting.

It's worth noting that many hosts will allow you to have SSH, but not at the root level. This is for updating your applications.

Getting ready

You will need the following:

1. You'll need direct SSH access to your server.
2. A copy of PuTTY or other terminal - PuTTY is available from:`http://www.chiark.greenend.org.uk/~sgtatham/PuTTY/download.html`
3. PuTTY comes in various flavors - pick the one that fits your desktop operating system.
4. You'll need your username and password for SSH to use PuTTY as well as your IP or server name

How to do it...

1. Install PuTTY on your local machine using the proper instructions for your OS.
2. Open PuTTY -- You'll see a screen that looks like the following:

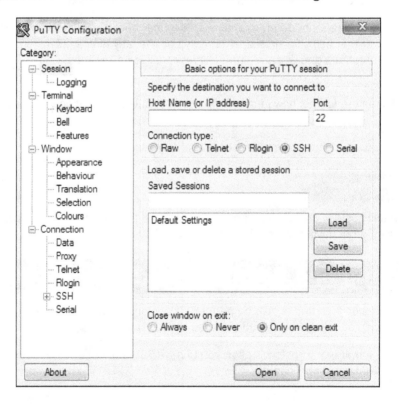

3. Fill in the **Host Name** and **Port** number (usually **22** is fine).
4. Click **Open** - you may get a message asking you if you want to accept the Key - say **Yes**.

5. Next you'll see this:

6. Enter your login name and your password.

7. You'll be logged in at this point:

```
root@host:~
login as: root
root@              password:
Last login: Sat Jul  3 16:22:39 2010 from

[root@host ~]#
[root@host ~]#
```

8. Type yum update.

   Yum is the updater for some of the more popular distributions of Linux. It will present a few downloads (if available) for installation. Just select YES to download and YES to install.

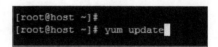

9. After you update, let's check the Apache web server.

10. Type httpd -v - In this case you see we are running (at time of writing) the latest and greatest).

```
[root@host ~]# httpd -v
Server version: Apache/2.2.15 (Unix)
Server built:   May 28 2010 11:54:04
Cpanel::Easy::Apache v3.2.0 rev5103
[root@host ~]#
```

11. You will need to verify your version against the current version(s) located at `httpd.apache.org`.

    Should you be out of date on this, it is suggested that you contact your host to update Apache for you.

    Be sure and conduct a full backup of the system using cPanel® or other means before attempting an update.

How it works...

Servers, like your desktop, have to stay updated. There are many other software stacks on a typical server that attackers can hit. These include the Kernel of the OS, supporting cast members like OpenSSL, Network services, PHP, MySQL, and many more.

The YUM updater is a tool that contacts good sources for Linux and other parts of the system updates. If they are available, it will handle the updating for you.

Index

Symbols

.htaccess file
  about 273
  protection, activating 272
  using, in Joomla! 272
  working 278
.tgz extension 66

A

Access Control List. *See* **ACL, Joomla! 1.6**
access level
  about 282, 289
  setting 290, 291
  setting, for module 301
ACL, Joomla! 1.6
  about 282
  access level 282-291
  article 282
  categories 282
  default groups 283
  global configuration 282
  group level access 285-287
  groups 282-288
  permission flow 283
  permissions 284
  users 282-288
  warning 282
administrative templates
  replacing 68-74
Agora forum
  about 141
  getting, to menu 143-146
  installing 142
  working 148-150

AllVideos plugin 215
article ACL 282
articles
  about 103, 114, 292
  assigning, to menu 127-132
  setting up 115-120
  tag, adding 223
  uploading 239

B

BEEZ default template 90
BlackWidow 273
blog
  parameters 141
  setting up, on Joomla! site 135-139
  working 140
blog articles 133
bots
  about 273
  blocking 273-276
  examples 273
browse 40

C

category
  about 103, 108
  comments, enabling 225
  creating 292, 293
  setting up 110-113
category ACL
  about 282
  best practices 299
category listings
  item view options 210-214

category manager
about 292
category, creating 292, 293
rules, accessing 295-299
screenshot 109
working 294

CCK
about 201
K2 202

chmod function 232, 237
commenting system 225, 226
comments
configuring 226
editing 228
enabling, by item 226
enabling, in category 225
moderating 226, 227
managing, on site 252, 253

CompojoomComment
about 248
comments, managing on site 252, 253
configuring 250, 251
downloading 248
installing 248
URL 248
working 249

component
about 187
disabling 192
installing 188-191
menu items, creating for 193, 194
uninstalling 191

configuration, CompojoomComment 250, 251
content
importing, into K2 203, 204
moderating 228
removing, from table 61-63
tagging 223, 224

Content Construction Kit. *See* **CCK**
Content Management System 48
content uploader extension
about 237
working 240

corn chart 58
cPanel® host
about 8

database, setting up 15-19
versus GoDaddy.com® 28-30
working 20

custom error page
adding 277

D

data 40
database
setting up, on cPanel® host 15-19
setting up, on GoDaddy.Com® server 20-24
table, removing 58-61
terms 40
working, phpMyAdmin used 53-57

database, terms
browse 40
data 40
drop 40
empty 40
export 40
import 40
row 40
table 40

default template 78
directories
ownership 265
permissions, setting for 268

DROP command 40, 47
DUMP 40

E

editor
about 98
selecting, for Joomla!1.5 100
TinyMCE 98

events
adding 244

export 40
exporting 41
extension manager
features 303
permissions 304

extensions 141, 187
eXtplorer
about 232
capabilities 232

control icons 233
directory, creating 235
downloading 232
file, creating 235
files, downloading 237
files, uploading 237
installing 232
local FTP authentication 234
permissions, changing 235-237
primary screen 232
working 233-237
extra field groups
adding 216
using 216
extra fields
adding 216
using 216

F

files
ownership 265
permissions, checking 35-38
permissions, setting for 269
FileZilla
about 8, 10, 234
starting 13
URL 9
working 15
folder
creating, in media manager 167
deleting 167, 168
permissions, checking 35-38
framework 187
FTP
settings 11
troubleshooting 265, 266
FTP program
installing 8
FTP program, installing
about 8
FileZilla, starting 13, 14
FTP, settings 11, 12
Joomla!, uncompressing 12
requisites 9, 10
steps 10, 11

G

GID number 56
GLOBAL ACL 283
global configuration 282
GoDaddy.Com® server
about 8
database, setting up 20-24
versus cPanel® host 28-30
working 24
Google crawler 273
group
about 282
and users 287, 288
assigning, to user 156
changing, of user 287, 288
permissions, changing 284
group level access 285-287

I

image
deleting 167, 168
IMPORT function
about 40
working 52
importing 48
index.php file 95
insert command 52
installation, Agora forum 142
installation, component 188-191
installation, eXtplorer 232
installation, FTP program
about 8
FileZilla, starting 13, 14
FTP, settings 11
Joomla!, uncompressing 12
requisites 9, 10
steps 10, 11
installation, JCE editor
about 100
com_jce_157_156_package.zip package,
selecting 100
installation, Joomla! 1.5
about 25
administration login screen 34
FTP, settings 30

license review 27
personalizing 31-33
pre-installation check 26
requisites 25
steps 25
working 35
installation, K2 202
installation, modules 196, 197
installation, template
Joomla! Administrator, used 66-68
manually 74-78
IP address
about 279
blocking 279, 280
item
comments, enabling 226
items AKA articles
about 217
working 218-221

J

JCE editor
about 98
assigning, to site 101-103
downloading 99
downloading, URL 99
installing 100
JCE editor, installing
about 100
com_jce_157_156_package.zip package,
    selecting 100
JomCalendar
about 241
as, menu item 245-247
using 242, 243
working 245
JomSocial 78
Joom!Fish 202
Joomla!
.htaccess file, using 272
about 187
administrative templates, replacing 68-74
CompojoomComment 248
content uploader extension 237-240
content uploader extension, configuring
    237-240

content uploader extension, using 237-240
core files, patching 270
eXtplorer 232
JomCalendar 241
requisites 8
template 65
troubleshooting 255
Joomla!1.5
editor, selecting 100
installing 25
password HASH generator 184-186
Joomla!1.5, installing
about 25
administration login screen 34
FTP, settings 30
license review 27
personalizing 31, 32, 33
pre-installation check 26
requisites 25
steps 25
Joomla!1.6
ACL 282
category manager 292-294
extensions manager 300
module manager 300-302
Joomla! Administrator
legacy mode 306, 307
template, installing 66-68
URL 66
Joomla! core files
patching 270
Joomla! site
about 267
AllVideos plugin 215
articles 114
articles, setting up 115-120
blog 133
blog, setting up 135-139
bots 273-276
categories 108
category, settting up 110-113
icon, changing 307, 308
JCE editor, assigning 101-103
K2, installing 202
Login module 169-174
lost super admin password 182-186
media manager 163, 164

menu, adding 125, 126
menus 124
multiple templates, using 78-84
permissions, setting 268
sections 103
sections, setting up 104-107
Simple Image Gallery PRO plugin 214
site contact, setting up 158
user management 151-154
web link manager 177-180
Joomlasphere 201
Joomla x tag 224

K

K2
commenting system 225, 226
content, importing 203, 204
downloading, URL 202
features 202
future configuration 205
installing 202
items AKA articles, working with 217-221
master categories, configuring 206, 207
master category 205
working 206
K2 Content Creation Kit x tag 224
K2 dashboard 204
K2, features
extra fields 215
extra groups 215
K2 icon 203
K2, installing 202
K2 Tag Cloud
about 222
example 222
image 222
K2 Tools module 222

L

legacy mode
activating 306, 307
deactivating 306, 307
working 307
Lipsum
URL 114

location
changing, for menu 194, 195
Login module
about 169
using 171-174
working 174
logo
replacing, in template 90-95

M

master category
about 205
category view options 209
configuring 206, 207
instructions 220
parameter settings 208, 209
MD5 186
media manager
about 163
features 165
folder, creating 167
media type, assigning 163, 164
media type, categorizing 163, 164
working 165
media manager tree
navigating, ways 165-167
menu
about 124
adding, to Joomla! site 125, 126
article, assigning for 127-132
location, changing 194, 195
menu items
creating, for components 193, 194
module manager
about 300
features 301, 302
working 301
module positions
about 65
determining, for templates 85-90
modules
about 187, 196
access levels, setting 301
creating 198-200
deleting, methods 197

disabling, methods 198
installing 196, 197
MySql 19
MySQL database
exporting, phpMyAdmin used 41-47
importing, phpMyAdmin used 48-52

N

new user
setting up, example 39

O

OPTIMIZE command
working 58

P

password HASH
creating 184, 185
patching
about 270
extensions 271
patching extensions 271
permissions
changing 235-237
allow command 284
changing, of groups 284
deny command 284
setting, for directories 268
setting, for files 269
setting, for site 268
php.ini file
about 277
site, protecting 277
working 278
phpMyAdmin
about 39
database, working 53-57
MySQL database, exporting 41-47
MySQL database, importing 48-52
PHP x tag 224
Pingdom
URL 167
public_html 10, 14, 269

PuTTY
installing 312
px size 210

R

rhuk_milky_way template 80
Rochen
URL 8
row 40
rules
accessing, of category manger 295-299

S

SALT 186
Search Engine Optimization. *See* **SEO**
sections
about 103
About Joomla! section 107
FAQs section 107
News section 107
setting up 104-107
secure session
using 147
SecureShell. *See* **SSH**
Security x tag 224
SEO 221
server signature
disabling 277
server software
checking 311-314
updating 311-314
shotgunning 255
Simple Image Gallery PRO plugin 214
site
comments, managing 252, 253
multiple calendars, displaying 246, 247
default contact, setting up 158-161
setting, for Tag Clouds 222
setting up, in subfolder 308
site contact
setting up 158
SSH
about 10
issues 264-266

super administrator account 157
super admin password
  forgot password 182, 183

T

table
  about 40
  content, removing 61-63
  removing, from database 58-61
tags
  about 221
  adding, to articles 223
  adding, to content 223, 224
  using, in K2 221
TAR function 237
template
  about 65
  administrative templates, replacing 68-74
  default template 78
  installing, Joomla! Administrator used 66-68
  installing, manually 74-78
  logo, replacing 90-95
  module positions, determining 85-90
  requisites 74
template providers
  URL 74
third-party developers
  com_securelive.zip 188
  mod_corephp_weather 188
third-party K2 template
  URL 208
third-party login module
  changing, to 175-177
timeout 48
TinyMCE editor
  about 98
  capabilities 98
  features 98
  screenshot 98
troubleshooting
  about 255
  extensions, installing 264
  extensions, reinstalling 264
  in, database connection 263, 264
  reasons 262
  working 261, 262

troubleshooting methodology
  developing 256-261
truncate command
  working 63

U

user accounts
  disabling 155
user management
  about 152
  example 154
  parameters, setting 153
  steps 153
users
  about 282
  and groups 287, 288
  deleting 155
  group, assigning 156
  group, changing 287, 288
  managing 152-154
  user accounts, disabling 155

V

var $dbprefix = 263
var $dbtype 263
var $host 263
var $password 263
var $user 263

W

web link manager
  about 177
  category, setting up 178-180
  link, setting up 178-180
  working 181, 182
WinZip® 12
WORD import function 98
WYSIWYG editor 241

Y

Yahoo! crawler 273

Z

Zeus 273

Thank you for buying
Joomla! 1.5 Cookbook

About Packt Publishing

Packt, pronounced 'packed', published its first book "*Mastering phpMyAdmin for Effective MySQL Management*" in April 2004 and subsequently continued to specialize in publishing highly focused books on specific technologies and solutions.

Our books and publications share the experiences of your fellow IT professionals in adapting and customizing today's systems, applications, and frameworks. Our solution based books give you the knowledge and power to customize the software and technologies you're using to get the job done. Packt books are more specific and less general than the IT books you have seen in the past. Our unique business model allows us to bring you more focused information, giving you more of what you need to know, and less of what you don't.

Packt is a modern, yet unique publishing company, which focuses on producing quality, cutting-edge books for communities of developers, administrators, and newbies alike. For more information, please visit our website: www.packtpub.com.

About Packt Open Source

In 2010, Packt launched two new brands, Packt Open Source and Packt Enterprise, in order to continue its focus on specialization. This book is part of the Packt Open Source brand, home to books published on software built around Open Source licences, and offering information to anybody from advanced developers to budding web designers. The Open Source brand also runs Packt's Open Source Royalty Scheme, by which Packt gives a royalty to each Open Source project about whose software a book is sold.

Writing for Packt

We welcome all inquiries from people who are interested in authoring. Book proposals should be sent to author@packtpub.com. If your book idea is still at an early stage and you would like to discuss it first before writing a formal book proposal, contact us; one of our commissioning editors will get in touch with you.

We're not just looking for published authors; if you have strong technical skills but no writing experience, our experienced editors can help you develop a writing career, or simply get some additional reward for your expertise.

open source

community experience distilled

Joomla! Web Security

ISBN: 978-1-847194-88-6   Paperback: 264 pages

Secure your Joomla! website from common security threats with this easy-to-use guide

1. Learn how to secure your Joomla! websites

2. Real-world tools to protect against hacks on your site

3. Implement disaster recovery features

4. Set up SSL on your site

5. Covers Joomla! 1.0 as well as 1.5

Joomla! 1.5 SEO

ISBN: 978-1-847198-16-7   Paperback: 324 pages

Improve the search engine friendliness of your web site

1. Improve the rankings of your Joomla! site in the search engine result pages such as Google, Yahoo, and Bing

2. Improve your web site SEO performance by gaining and producing incoming links to your web site

3. Market and measure the success of your blog by applying SEO

4. Integrate analytics and paid advertising into your Joomla! blog

Please check **www.PacktPub.com** for information on our titles

Joomla! 1.5 Development Cookbook

ISBN: 978-1-847198-14-3   Paperback: 360 pages

Solve real world Joomla! 1.5 development problems with over 130 simple but incredibly useful recipes

1. Simple but incredibly useful solutions to real world Joomla! 1.5 development problems

2. Rapidly extend the Joomla! core functionality to create new and exciting extension

3. Hands-on solutions that takes a practical approach to recipes - providing code samples that can easily be extracted

Joomla! 1.5 Template Design

ISBN: 978-1-847197-16-0   Paperback: 284 pages

Improve the search engine friendliness of your web site

1. Create Joomla! 1.5 Templates for your sites

2. Debug, validate, and package your templates

3. Tips for tweaking existing templates with Flash, extensions and JavaScript libraries

Please check **www.PacktPub.com** for information on our titles